THE TIMES
TOP 100
GRADUATE EMPLOYERS

The definitive guide to the leading employers
recruiting graduates during 2007-2008.

HIGH FLIERS

**HIGH FLIERS PUBLICATIONS LTD
IN ASSOCIATION WITH THE TIMES**

Published by High Fliers Publications Limited
King's Gate, 1 Bravingtons Walk, London N1 9AE
Telephone: 020 7428 9100   Web: www.Top100GraduateEmployers.com

Editor Martin Birchall
Publisher Gill Thomas
Production Manager Robin Burrows
Portrait Photography Sarah Merson

The Times Top 100 Graduate Employers is based on research results
from The UK Graduate Careers Survey 2007, produced by High Fliers
Research Ltd.

The greatest care has been taken in compiling this book. However, no
responsibility can be accepted by the publishers or compilers for the
accuracy of the information presented.

Where opinion is expressed it is that of the author or advertiser and
does not necessarily coincide with the editorial views of High Fliers
Publications Limited or The Times newspaper.

Printed and bound in Italy by L.E.G.O. S.p.A.

A CIP catalogue record for this book
is available from the British Library.
ISBN 978-0-9536991-8-6

Contents

Information Request Service

Find out more about Britain's top employers and you could win
an iPod nano (PROJECT) RED or start your career £5,000 richer!

Foreword

by Martin Birchall
Editor, The Times Top 100 Graduate Employers

Welcome to the latest edition of *The Times Top 100 Graduate Employers*, your guide to the UK's leading employers who are recruiting graduates in 2007-2008. If you're one of the quarter of a million final year university students due to graduate in the summer of 2008, then the employment outlook is extremely encouraging. The employers featured within the *Top 100* hired record numbers of graduates in 2006-2007 and are set to recruit even larger numbers this year.

At least 600 major employers in the UK currently operate a recognised graduate recruitment scheme and promote their vacancies to university students. In addition, there are literally hundreds of small and medium-sized businesses that also recruit graduates into their organisations, often from local universities. This means that up to 250 different recruiters are expected to hold recruitment events or take part in campus careers fairs at many of the universities most popular with employers.

Given such a wide choice of different types of employment and graduate jobs, how can prospective employers be assessed and ranked?

To find out, we interviewed over 17,000 final year students who graduated from universities across the UK in the summer of 2007, and asked them "Which employer do you think offers the best opportunities for graduates?" Between them, the 'Class of 2007' named organisations from every imaginable employment sector and business type – from the 'Big Four' accounting & professional services firms to manufacturers, investment banks to government departments, leading charities to well-known IT companies and consulting firms. The one hundred employers who were mentioned most often during the research form *The Times Top 100 Graduate Employers*.

This book is therefore a celebration of the employers who are judged to offer the brightest prospects for graduates. Whether by the quality of their training programmes, the business success that they enjoy, the scale of their organisations, or by the impression that their recruitment promotions have made – these are the employers that are most attractive to university-leavers in 2007.

The Times Top 100 Graduate Employers will not necessarily identify which organisation is right for you: only you can decide that. But it is an invaluable reference if you want to discover which graduate jobs Britain's leading employers offer.

Leaving university and finding your first job can be a daunting process but it is one of the most important steps you'll ever take. Having a good understanding of the range of opportunities available must be the best way to start.

Martin Birchall writes a weekly Top 100 column for 'Career', the jobs & employment section of The Times.

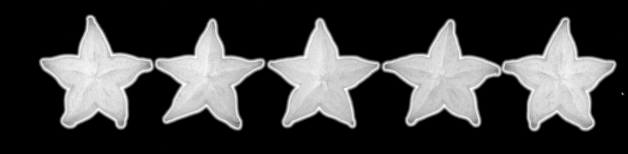

If you have 5-star quality,
here's your chance to shine.

If you want the best – and are the best – you'll appreciate and deserve the freedom to determine your own career and the speed of its progression. You'll want the licence to make your own mistakes – and learn the valuable lessons from them. And you'll be pleased to know that we're searching out our next generation of the brightest stars – and offering them a place on the Aldi Graduate Area Manager Training Programme.

"Three years at Aldi has felt like three minutes. Everything is so fast paced – and I've been flat out busy all that time. But I wouldn't want it any other way, because the diversity and responsibility of this job excites and challenges me every day of the week." Sandy Mitchell, Area Manager.

"Even though this is very much Aldi's Graduate Recruitment Scheme, they always give you the chance to express your individualism and your own ideas. And being given such responsibility at such an early stage really gives you the chance to shine." Zoe Witowski, Area Manager.

Find out more on Page 62.

ALDI

Compiling the Top 100 Graduate Employers

by Gill Thomas
Publisher, High Fliers Publications Ltd

Final year students or graduates who've left university recently certainly have a wide choice of prospective employers at the moment. Entry-level vacancies at Britain's best-known organisations have risen by more than 50 per cent over the last five years and there are expected to be over five thousand organisations competing to hire the best graduates from UK universities during the 2007-2008 recruitment season.

Such a huge choice can make selecting the employer that is 'right' for you much more difficult. How should you evaluate all the different opportunities and what determines which employers offer the best graduate positions? What are the main criteria that you can use to assess so many organisations and jobs?

There are no simple answers to these questions and clearly no single individual employer can ever hope to be right for every graduate – everyone makes their own judgements about the organisations they want to work for and the type of job they find the most attractive.

So how can anyone produce a meaningful league table of Britain's leading graduate employers? What criteria can define whether one organisation is 'better' than another? To compile *The Times Top 100 Graduate Employers*, the independent market research company, High Fliers Research Ltd, interviewed 17,170 final year students who left UK universities in the summer of 2007. These students from the 'Class of 2007' who took part in the study were selected at random to represent the full cross-section of finalists at their universities, not just those who had already secured graduate employment. The research examined students' experiences during their search for a graduate job and asked them about their attitudes to employers.

The key question used to produce the *Top 100* was "Which employer do you think offers the best opportunities for graduates?" This question was deliberately open-ended and students were not prompted in any way. Across the whole survey, finalists mentioned more than 600 different organisations – from the smallest local employers, to some of the world's best-known companies. The responses were analysed to identify the number of times each employer was mentioned. The one hundred organisations that were mentioned most often are the *The Times Top 100 Graduate Employers* for 2007.

It is clear from the considerable selection of answers given by finalists from the 'Class of 2007' that individual students used very different criteria to determine which employer they considered offered the best opportunities for graduates. Some focused on employers' general reputations – their public image, their business profile or their commercial success. Others evaluated employers based on the information they had

The Top 100 Graduate Employers 2007

This Year	Last Year		This Year	Last Year	
1.	1	PricewaterhouseCoopers	51.	54	Foreign Office
2.	2	Deloitte	52.	55	Eversheds
3.	3	KPMG	53.	45	Oxfam
4.	4	Civil Service	54.	72	John Lewis
5.	5	BBC	55.	57	Freshfields Bruckhaus Deringer
6.	6	NHS	56.	80	Bloomberg
7.	8	Accenture	57.	58	Arup
8.	7	HSBC	58.	79	Slaughter and May
9.	12	Aldi	59.	68	Lehman Brothers
10.	10	Goldman Sachs	60.	62	WPP
11.	14	Ernst & Young	61.	52	ASDA
12.	11	Shell	62.	92	Pfizer
13.	17	GlaxoSmithKline	63.	63	ExxonMobil
14.	16	Teach First	64.	64	Lovells
15.	9	Procter & Gamble	65.	69	Reuters
16.	15	Royal Bank of Scotland Group	66.	65	Bain & Company
17.	22	Marks & Spencer	67.	47	Cadbury Schweppes
18.	13	Army	68.	90	Baker & McKenzie
19.	20	BP	69.	61	HBOS
20.	31	UBS	70.	50	Royal Navy
21.	18	IBM	71.	75	Credit Suisse
22.	19	JPMorgan	72.	74	Corus
23.	21	Unilever	73.	89	Saatchi & Saatchi
24.	23	Rolls-Royce	74.	NEW	BDO Stoy Hayward
25.	27	Police	75.	46	Alliance Boots
26.	26	Tesco	76.	67	Mercer
27.	35	Barclays Bank	77.	70	GCHQ
28.	44	Linklaters	78.	86	British Airways
29.	33	Deutsche Bank	79.	71	McDonald's Restaurants
30.	28	L'Oréal	80.	81	Fujitsu
31.	41	Allen & Overy	81.	NEW	GE
32.	34	Citi	82.	49	Diageo
33.	25	Morgan Stanley	83.	93	Financial Services Authority
34.	24	Microsoft	84.	78	Boston Consulting Group
35.	38	RAF	85.	91	Herbert Smith
36.	56	Merrill Lynch	86.	94	Penguin
37.	30	McKinsey & Company	87.	NEW	npower
38.	32	Mars	88.	NEW	Maersk
39.	53	Google	89.	NEW	Transport for London
40.	39	Local Government	90.	NEW	Faber Maunsell
41.	43	BAE Systems	91.	100	Addleshaw Goddard
42.	29	BT	92.	96	Bank of America
43.	59	Atkins	93.	83	DLA Piper
44.	36	AstraZeneca	94.	84	Environment Agency
45.	40	Clifford Chance	95.	NEW	ABN AMRO
46.	73	Barclays Capital	96.	NEW	MI5 – The Security Service
47.	51	Arcadia Group	97.	82	Intel
48.	66	Cancer Research UK	98.	NEW	Capgemini
49.	37	Lloyds TSB	99.	NEW	Norton Rose
50.	42	Sainsbury's	100.	NEW	The Co-operative Group

Source **The UK Graduate Careers Survey 2007**, High Fliers Research Ltd. 17,170 final year students leaving UK universities in the summer of 2007 were asked 'Which employer do you think offers the best opportunities for graduates?'

seen during their job search – the quality of recruitment promotions, the impression formed from meeting employers' representatives, or experiences through the recruitment and selection process. Finalists also considered the level of vacancies that organisations were recruiting for as an indicator of possible employment prospects, or were influenced by employers' profile on campus.

Many students, however, used the 'employment proposition' as their main guide – the quality of graduate training and development that an employer offers, the remuneration package available, and the practical aspects of a first job such as location or working hours.

Regardless of the criteria that students used to arrive at their answer, the hardest part for many was just selecting a single organisation. To some extent, choosing two or three, or even half a dozen employers would have been much easier. But the whole purpose of the exercise was to replicate the reality that everyone faces – you can only work for one organisation. And at each stage of the job search there are choices to be made as to which direction to take and which employers to pursue.

The resulting *Top 100* is a dynamic league table of the UK's most exciting and well-respected graduate recruiters in 2007. For a fourth consecutive year, the accounting & professional services firm Pricewaterhouse-Coopers has been voted the UK's top graduate recruiter. Just over 10 per cent of finalists thought the firm – which is currently one of Britain's largest graduate employers – offered the best opportunities for university-leavers in 2007. And for the second year running, the top three places are all taken by 'Big Four' professional services firms – Deloitte and KPMG remain in 2nd and 3rd places respectively.

The Civil Service, BBC and NHS are also unchanged in 4th, 5th and 6th places but consulting firm Accenture has moved up one place to 7th position, overtaking HSBC which slips back to 8th. Discount retailer Aldi has entered the top ten for the first time and is ranked in 9th place this year, continuing its rapid rise up the rankings since entering the *Top 100* in 65th place in 2002. The top-rated investment bank Goldman Sachs is ranked in 10th position for a second year.

Elsewhere in the top twenty, there have been several significant changes. Ernst & Young, the accounting & professional services firm and GlaxoSmithKline each move up, to 11th and 13th respectively and Teach First – the scheme that recruits talented graduates into teaching before embarking on careers in other areas – achieves its highest ranking to date in 14th place. However, Procter & Gamble, the consumer goods company, drops six places to 15th position, leaving the top ten rankings for the first time. Shell and the Royal Bank of Scotland Group each slip one place and the Army drops a further five places to 18th. Marks & Spencer climbs five places to rejoin the top twenty in 17th place and UBS jumps from outside last year's top thirty to 20th place. Both IBM and JPMorgan have left the top twenty.

The three highest climbers in 2007 are Pfizer which has jumped thirty places, reversing a similar fall last year, Barclays Capital moves into the top fifty with a climb of twenty-seven places, and information and media group Bloomberg is up twenty-four places to 56th position. Heading in the wrong direction, the biggest falls of the year are for drinks company Diageo which drops thirty-three places, Alliance Boots is down twenty-nine places, and Cadbury Schweppes and the Royal Navy both fall twenty places in the new league table.

There have been mixed fortunes for the law firms in the *Top 100*. Linklaters has climbed sixteen places, overtaking Clifford Chance to become the highest-ranking law firm this year. Allen & Overy has gone up ten places and two firms – Slaughter and May and Baker & McKenzie – have both climbed more than twenty places. Within the investment banks the results are also varied – Deutsche Bank, Merrill Lynch, Citi, Lehman Brothers, Credit Suisse and the Bank of America have each improved their *Top 100* rankings, but Morgan Stanley has slipped from the top thirty.

There are a total of eleven new entries in this year's *Top 100*, the highest being for accounting & professional services firm BDO Stoy Hayward in 74th place. International conglomerate, the GE corporation appear in 81st place, energy group npower joins the list in 87th place, just ahead of shipping group Maersk, Transport for London and construction firm Faber Maunsell.

There are further new entries for consultants Capgemini and The Co-operative Group. Three employers return to the league table – the investment bank ABN AMRO, MI5 - The Security Service and law firm Norton Rose.

Among the organisations leaving the Top 100 in 2007 are defence employer QinetiQ – which was ranked inside last year's top fifty – and the Ministry of Defence and Dstl. Data Connection, one of the highest climbers in 2006 has left the list, as have Siemens, Airbus and Sony. Four of last year's new entries also failed to retain their places – Virgin, Grant Thornton, the Nationwide Building Society and the Government Legal Service.

This year's edition of *The Times Top 100 Graduate Employers* has produced a number of significant changes, particularly towards the top of the list, and the results provide a unique insight into how graduates from the 'Class of 2007' rated the leading employers in 2006-2007. Many of these organisations are featured in the 'Employer Entry' section of this book. Starting on page 53, you can see a two-page profile for each employer, listed alphabetically for easy reference.

The editorial part of the entry includes a short description of what the organisation does, its opportunities for graduates and its recruitment programme for 2007-2008. A fact file for each employer gives details of the number of graduate vacancies, the business functions that graduates are recruited for, likely starting salaries for 2008, application deadlines, the universities that the employer is intending to visit during the year, and contact details for their recruitment website and graduate brochure. The right-hand page of the entry contains a display advert from the employer.

If you would like to find out more about any of the employers featured in *The Times Top 100 Graduate Employers*, then you can use the book's 'Information Request Service' – simply register your personal details and the employers you are interested in using the request card that appears opposite page 224, or go online to **www.Top100GraduateEmployers.com**

You'll receive email bulletins about the employers, details of their presentations and careers events at your university, and other information about their graduate recruitment. The service is entirely free and you choose which organisations you would like to hear about.

Using the 'Information Request Service' enters you into a prize draw to win **£5,000**. There are also 50 **iPod Nanos** (PRODUCT) RED to be won – one at each of the universities at which *The Times Top 100 Graduate Employers* book is distributed – for those who return information request cards before **30th November 2007**.

THE TIMES
TOP 100
GRADUATE EMPLOYERS

Employers in this year's Top 100

		Number of Employers			Number of Employers
1.	Investment Bank	12	9.	Bank or Financial Institution	5
2.	Law Firm	12	10.	Accountancy or Professional Services Firm	5
3.	Public Sector Employer	11	11.	Consulting Firm	5
4.	Retailer	10	12.	Armed Forces	3
5.	Engineering or Industrial Company	8	13.	Oil Company	3
6.	IT or Telecoms Company	7	14.	Chemical or Pharmaceutical Company	3
7.	Fast-Moving Consumer Goods Company	6	15.	Charity or Voluntary Sector	2
8.	Media Company	6	16.	Other	2

Source **The UK Graduate Careers Survey 2007**, High Fliers Research Ltd. 17,170 final year students leaving UK universities in the summer 2007 were asked 'Which employer do you think offers the best opportunities for graduates?'

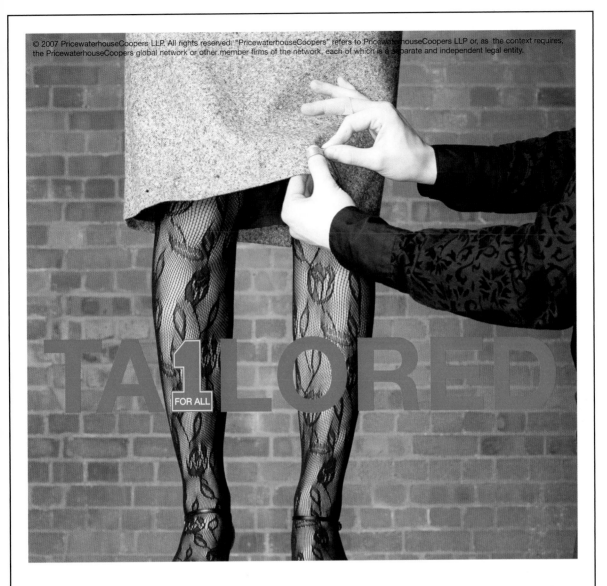

TA1LORED
FOR ALL

**Nationwide Opportunities
Spring and Autumn 2008**

Assurance
Tax
Advisory
Actuarial
Strategy

We'll give you the encouragement, support and tailored development you need to design your own career path. That's why our development training programmes are flexible enough to cater for people who want to specialise in one specific business area as well as those keen to get a variety of experience. And whatever's right for you, we'll make sure you pick up the key technical, business and personal skills you need to progress. For a career that will fit you perfectly just bring us a 2:1 in any subject, at least a 280 UCAS tariff or equivalent, and plenty of enthusiasm and ideas. We're the one firm for all smart graduates.

www.pwc.com/uk/careers/

Text: PwC to 85792

We value diversity in our people.

Tackling complicated situations with ingenuity. Just another day at the office for a Tiger.

At Accenture, we relish the opportunity to solve problems, push back the boundaries and do what hasn't been tried before. We're one of the world's leading management consulting, technology services and outsourcing companies and we want talented people who are looking for a challenge. Join our global team and you'll be delivering the innovation that helps our clients become high-performance businesses.

Internships and placements in consulting

We have a range of schemes and placements for up-and-coming talent who want to put their skills to the test sooner. You could combine work experience with a few months' travel during your pre-university gap year on our Horizons Scheme. You could get a better understanding of what we do on our Summer Vacation Scheme, or get involved with real projects on our six or twelve-month Industrial Placement.

Perhaps you're looking for a taste of business and IT Consulting? You could also take part in our Navigator Scheme after you graduate or The Sampler—a one day insight into the world of Accenture.

Whatever the scheme, you will find a business that gives you the chance to develop skills in many different ways.

Through a range of initiatives here in the UK and in many other countries, our people take part in projects that affect communities, organisations and individuals.

To find out more, visit our website. Accenture is committed to being an equal opportunities employer.

Visit accenture.com/ukschemes

• Consulting • Technology • Outsourcing

High performance. Delivered.

THE TIMES
TOP 100
GRADUATE EMPLOYERS

TOP 100 GRADUATE EMP
TOP 100 GRADUATE EMF
TOP 100 GRADUATE EMF
TOP 100 GRADUATE EMP
TOP 100 GRADUATE EMF
TOP 100 GRADUATE EMI
TOP 100 GRADUATE EM
TOP 100 GRADUATE EN
TOP 100 GRADUATE EM
TOP 100 GRADUATE EM
TOP 100 GRADUATE EMI
TOP 100 GRADUATE EM
TOP 100 GRADUATE EM
TOP 100 GRADUATE EMI
TOP 100 GRADUATE EMP
TOP 100 GRADUATE EMPI
TOP 100 GRADUATE EMPL
TOP 100 GRADUATE EMPL
TOP 100 GRADUATE EMPL
TOP 100 GRADUATE EMPL
TOP 100 GRADUATE EMPL
TOP 100 CRADUATE EMPL

The Times Graduate Recruitment Awards

As well as *The Times Top 100 Graduate Employers* league table, students from the 'Class of 2007' were also asked about the 'graduate employers of choice' within individual career sectors.

Finalists who were actively applying for graduate jobs in sixteen separate areas, such as engineering, IT, finance, human resources, sales and marketing etc, were asked the open-ended question 'Which employer would you most like to work for?'.

The winners of *The Times Graduate Recruitment Awards 2007* are listed here:

Source **The UK Graduate Careers Survey 2007**, High Fliers Research Ltd. 17,170 final year students leaving university in the summer 2007 were asked 'Which employer do you most want to work for?' within the career sectors they had applied to.

How to Use the Directory

Many of the employers listed within *The Times Top 100 Graduate Employers* are featured in the 'Employer Entries' section of the directory. These entries describe what each organisation does, the opportunities they offer graduates, and practical details about their recruitment programme for 2007-2008.

The 'Employer Entry' section begins on **page 53**.

Each entry follows a standard format, and contains two elements: descriptive text and easy-to-find information on the employer's vacancies, contact details and salary expectations.

Locations of jobs
The regional locations of the employer's jobs are highlighted in red.

Vacancies
The number of likely graduate vacancies at this employer in 2007-2008

Career areas recruited for
Details of the generic career areas that the employer recruits into. There are 17 areas to look out for:

Accountancy
Consulting
Engineering
Finance
General Management
Human Resources
Investment Banking
IT
Law
Logistics
Manufacturing
Marketing
Media
Purchasing
Research & Development
Retailing
Sales

Employer's graduate recruitment website

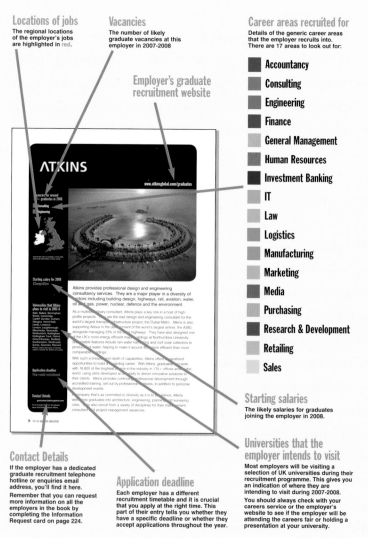

Starting salaries
The likely salaries for graduates joining the employer in 2008.

Universities that the employer intends to visit
Most employers will be visiting a selection of UK universities during their recruitment programme. This gives you an indication of where they are intending to visit during 2007-2008. You should always check with your careers service or the employer's website to see if the employer will be attending the careers fair or holding a presentation at your university.

Contact Details
If the employer has a dedicated graduate recruitment telephone hotline or enquiries email address, you'll find it here. Remember that you can request more information on all the employers in the book by completing the Information Request card on page 224.

Application deadline
Each employer has a different recruitment timetable and it is crucial that you apply at the right time. This part of their entry tells you whether they have a specific deadline or whether they accept applications throughout the year.

AMAZING CAREER AWAITS.

It's no wonder that many of today's business and financial superstars are ACA-qualified. Around the world, the ACA inspires business confidence. It can do the same for you.

It's not just us who say so: a recent independent survey showed that ACAs are in demand in a large number of business sectors and are much prized (average salary packages top £100,000). And they rise high: 67% of FTSE 100 qualified accountants acting as Finance Director or CEO have an ACA (that's more than four times the number holding any other single qualification).

Inspire confidence with the ACA qualification.

W **www.icaew.com/careers**
T   **+44 (0)1908 248 040**
E   **careers@icaew.com**

ICAEW

**THE INSTITUTE
OF CHARTERED
ACCOUNTANTS**
IN ENGLAND AND WALES

Graduate opportunities, all disciplines.

If you want a career that offers more of the things that really count, welcome to AstraZeneca. We turn good ideas into effective medicines and our innovation enhances the lives of patients around the world.

If you're a graduate with serious talent and big ambitions, you'll never be just another face in the crowd. Our approach to development is focused on giving you the support you need to reach your potential – and rewarding your performance as an individual.

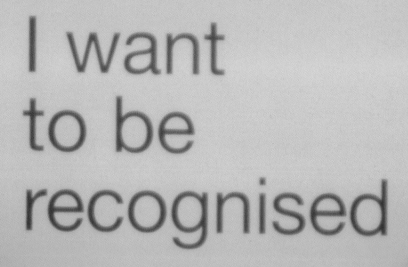

Find the recognition you deserve at
ideas.astrazeneca.com
sign up for job alerts and let the opportunities come to you

AstraZeneca
life inspiring ideas

Understanding the Graduate Market

by Carol Lewis
Editor, Career - The Times

Just as need and desirability are drivers for our purchases in the high street, so they play their role in the graduate job market. Employers, who want to hire university leavers, need to make themselves desirable to graduates. Graduates, who want to be hired, need to make themselves appealing to employers. The ideal market for graduates is lots of employers who want to hire lots of talented university-leavers. The best market situation for employers is lots of bright well-rounded university leavers looking for jobs.

In the last ten years the number of people graduating from university has risen dramatically and last year there were estimated to be about 260,000 graduates. And yet for these 260,000 people there were fewer than 90,000 graduate level vacancies. A quick bit of arithmetic shows that is the equivalent of one job for every three graduates.

Of course not everyone wants a graduate job – some will want to travel, study, volunteer or find employment in roles which aren't strictly graduate jobs. Nonetheless getting a place on a good graduate development programme at a top-notch employer isn't easy with vacancies for the most desirable jobs attracting up to a hundred applications each.

The good news is that graduate vacancies at *The Times Top 100 Employers* are set to increase by almost 12 per cent this year compared to just over 10 per cent in 2007. Together the employers featured in this year's *Top 100* are set to hire 18,687 graduates, compared to the 16,711 recruited during 2006-2007.

The average number of graduate vacancies at *Top 100* employers in 2008 is 200 per organisation. One in ten employers plan to hire at least 500 new recruits and three employers anticipate hiring at least 1,000 university leavers. This means working for one of these major employers not only offers career enhancing professional development, but access to a wide-ranging peer network – which is a valuable commodity in a society which rewards the well connected.

More than two-fifths of the leading employers plan to hire more graduates this recruitment season than last, half believe they will recruit similar numbers to 2007, while just one in ten expects to reduce their overall graduate intake in 2008.

This is all good news, particularly for those with a head for figures – most of the vacancies are at accountancy firms (23.8 per cent of total graduate jobs) or investment banks (19 per cent of total). Don't panic if you are an arts graduate though: almost all the big professional services firms and financial institutions say they want to recruit people from a broad range of degree backgrounds – they are not looking to just hire ready-made accountants and bankers.

If you once imagined yourself as a rock 'n' roll legend…

…don't worry. You can still make a name for yourself in the music business.

Aspirations drive individuals and businesses. By constantly fulfilling ours, we've kept ahead in the global marketplace for professional services. It's the aspiration and ambitions of exceptional individuals like you that have helped us achieve our goals.

For you, a childhood dream of playing to stadium crowds could become the reality of providing vital business advice to some of the biggest names in the music business.

Wherever your aspirations take you within Deloitte, you'll have the promise of a career that can take you further – and faster – than you ever thought possible.

www.deloitte.co.uk/graduates

A career worth aspiring to

Deloitte.

Audit . Tax . Consulting . Corporate Finance .

The employers who intend to hire the fewest graduates are those in the chemical & pharmaceutical sector (0.3 per cent of total graduate jobs), consumer goods (1.7 per cent), and media (1.7 per cent).

The fastest growing sectors are the high street banks and financial employers, with graduate vacancies up by 31.4 per cent, investment banks (vacancies up 28.4 per cent), consulting firms (up by 19.6 per cent) and retailers (up 19 per cent). All the other major career destinations are expecting to take on additional graduates in 2008 with the exception of law firms which anticipate hiring similar numbers to 2007 and the Armed Forces and the media where vacancies are predicted to fall.

The biggest graduate recruiters in *The Times Top 100 Graduate Employers* during 2007-2008 are PricewaterhouseCoopers and Deloitte (1,200 vacancies each), KPMG (1,000 vacancies),

Ernst & Young (750 vacancies), the Army and Barclays Capital (600 vacancies each), the RBS Group (550 vacancies), Accenture and the Civil Service (500 vacancies each).

The majority of chief executives of UK FTSE100 companies come from a background of working in financial management according to a study by Dr Elizabeth Marx, a partner at headhunters Heidrick and Struggles, which suggests the current crop of graduate jobs really could be the first rung on the ladder to a stellar career.

More than half of the *Top 100* companies have graduate vacancies in financial management and IT, a third offer jobs in sales and marketing, a quarter of employers are hiring graduate engineers or general managers and a fifth are looking for research & development personnel.

Just nine organisations have media vacancies. The media is always one of the most desirable career destinations for graduates, this suggests

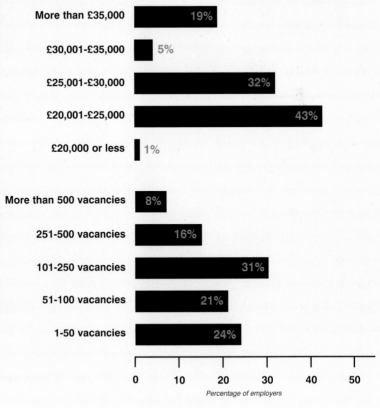

THE TIMES

TOP 100
GRADUATE EMPLOYERS

Graduate Salaries & Vacancies in 2008

More than £35,000	19%
£30,001-£35,000	5%
£25,001-£30,000	32%
£20,001-£25,000	43%
£20,000 or less	1%
More than 500 vacancies	8%
251-500 vacancies	16%
101-250 vacancies	31%
51-100 vacancies	21%
1-50 vacancies	24%

0   10   20   30   40   50
Percentage of employers

Source **The Times Top 100 Graduate Employers 2007-8**, High Fliers Research Ltd. Average graduate starting salaries and total number of graduate vacancies in 2008 at the organisations featured in The Times Top 100 Graduate Employers.

that graduates intent on pursuing media careers would do well to consider applying to employers outside the *Top 100* or looking for vacancies that are not specifically classified as graduate jobs.

A recent survey by High Fliers Research of more than 17,000 final year students expecting to graduate in 2007 showed that most wanted to work in London and the south of England. Let's hope the same is true in 2008 because four-fifths of leading employers are recruiting graduates to work in the capital and nearly half have vacancies in the south east of England, the Midlands or the North West. By contrast, only around a third have any vacancies in Scotland, Wales or Northern Ireland. The region with the fewest graduate employers is East Anglia.

Obviously everyone wants an interesting and satisfying career but the fiscal reality is that with the average student leaving university £10,000 in debt salaries do matter. Luckily the UK's leading

graduate employers are boosting starting salaries by 6.3 per cent in 2008, taking average packages to £25,500 – a £1,500 increase on last year's average graduate starting salary.

More than a quarter of the top graduate programmes will now pay graduates at least £30,000 when they start work. The most generous salaries tend to be those on offer from investment banks (an average of £38,000), law firms (an average of £36,000), and consulting firms (an average of £31,000), each of which have increased substantially compared to last year.

There is much more to life than money though and graduates really need to consider what motivates them, what career development and training opportunities are available, the work-life balance they want and their long-term career strategies. None of the *Top 100* employers which publish starting salary details are paying less than £17,000 to their new graduates.

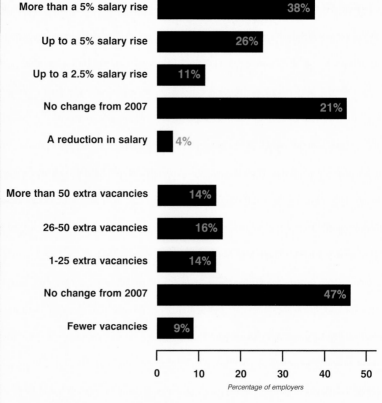

THE TIMES
TOP 100
GRADUATE EMPLOYERS

Changes to Salaries & Vacancies in 2008

More than a 5% salary rise	38%
Up to a 5% salary rise	26%
Up to a 2.5% salary rise	11%
No change from 2007	21%
A reduction in salary	4%
More than 50 extra vacancies	14%
26-50 extra vacancies	16%
1-25 extra vacancies	14%
No change from 2007	47%
Fewer vacancies	9%

0   10   20   30   40   50
Percentage of employers

Source **The Times Top 100 Graduate Employers 2007-8**, High Fliers Research Ltd. Graduate starting salaries & vacancy levels in 2008, compared with recruitment in 2007 at the organisations featured in The Times Top 100 Graduate Employers

global reputation

[**limitless potential**]

growth and success

inspiring colleagues

Merrill Lynch is one of the world's leading wealth management, capital markets and advisory companies. Our iconic brand and global capabilities offer you the chance to realise your potential whilst working side-by-side with thought leaders on projects of breathtaking scope and complexity. Join us and you can also benefit from a performance-based culture of excellence, where respect for the individual, commitment to breakthrough, big-picture thinking and enduring values create an environment for your continued growth and success.

For more information or to apply online, visit
ml.com/careers/europe

Merrill Lynch is an equal opportunity employer.

THE SUNDAY TIMES
100
BEST COMPANIES
TO WORK FOR **2007**

ml.com/careers/europe

Merrill Lynch

There are plenty of employers looking to hire talented university leavers and to get a slice of the action graduates need to get out and sell themselves to their chosen organisations. The majority of leading employers are not that hard to find – most of *The Times Top 100 Employers* are actively marketing their graduate vacancies at between 15 and 20 UK universities this year. Companies use a variety of careers fairs, campus recruitment presentations and media advertising. The universities likely to host the most events run by Britain's leading graduate employers in 2007-2008 are Manchester, Cambridge, London, Oxford, Nottingham, Warwick and Bristol.

But if the company you'd most like to work for isn't visiting your university then don't despair, log on instead – every major employer has its own website which will give full details about their graduate recruitment programmes, often complete with case studies. What is more, most employers will accept work experience and graduate applications online.

Half of the UK's top employers now recruit all the year-round and will accept applications throughout the 2007-2008 recruitment season. For employers with a single application deadline, the most common deadlines are in November or December, although law firms usually have July closing dates.

To recap, there are lots of reasons to feel positive about life after graduation – vacancies for university leavers have now risen by more than 50 per cent since 2004 and starting salaries for new graduates have increased by an impressive 15 per cent over the same period.

No one can expect to walk into a job; there is tough competition for all vacancies and the leading employers have rigorous selection procedures which include psychometric testing. Graduates not only need to gain a good degree – most of the top employers want to recruit those with a first or 2.1 – but also pick up vital soft skills along the way; employers crave well-rounded individuals with demonstrable competencies such as communication skills, motivation and organisation, the ability to work in teams and leadership potential.

But for those finalists who do make the grade though there are rewarding careers and some great starting salaries on offer at *The Times Top 100 Graduate Employers*.

'Career' is the weekly jobs section published every Thursday in The Times – www.timesonline.co.uk/career

Graduate Employment in 2008, by Industry

	2007		% of total vacancies in 2008	How graduate vacancies compare with 2007
1.	1	Accountancy or Professional Services Firms	23.8	Up 8.5%
2.	2	Investment Banks or Fund Managers	19.0	Up 28.4%
3.	5	Engineering or Industrial Companies	8.6	Up 9.5%
4.	4	Public Sector	8.3	Up 17.4%
5.	6	Banking or Financial Services	7.2	Up 31.4%
6.	8	Retailers	5.7	Up 19.0%
7.	7	Law Firms	5.7	Up 1.2%
8.	3	Armed Forces	5.2	Down 29.2%
9.	9	IT & Telecommunications Companies	4.3	Up 3.9%
10.	11	Consulting Firms	3.3	Up 19.6%
11.	12	Oil & Energy Companies	2.9	Up 57.1%
12.	10	Media Organisations	2.7	Down 23.1%
13.	13	Consumer Goods Manufacturers	1.7	Up 33.8%
14.	14	Chemical & Pharmaceuticals	0.3	Up 8.3%
15.	-	Other	1.3	-

Source **The Times Top 100 Graduate Employers 2007-8**, High Fliers Research Ltd. Graduate vacancy levels in 2008, compared with total numbers recruited in 2007 at the organisations featured in The Times Top 100 Graduate Employers

" Only my Mum has a higher opinion of me"

We think that everyone needs encouragement and support to become truly great at what they do. What gets you here in the first place is just the start – no one thinks our people have more potential than we do. Except, maybe, their mum and dad.

www.ey.com/uk/careers

RWE Group

Who makes sure the
loudest bands
get the green light?

From rock to reggae, metal to mod, Wembley Stadium has been home to some of the biggest bands in history. So, when we were asked to provide the power for the famous arch, we needed to make sure we were completely in tune with the planet. The solution was a unique renewable energy contract that ensures we match our normal supply with electricity provided by our own windfarms on the coast. Meaning that even when some of the bands' lyrics are a little blue, we can honestly say we stay green.

It's this sort of thinking that our graduates face every day. And why we're looking for talented, bright people to join us in engineering, commercial and risk, finance, HR, on our IS scheme within our systems division or as a business generalist (not the snappiest lyrics in the world we agree, but we had to tell you what careers are on offer).

If you fancy blowing your own trumpet, visit (www.brightergraduates.com) to find out more.

Successful Job Hunting

by Gordon Chesterman
Director, Cambridge University Careers Service

If you're trying to work out the answer to the question "What the heck am I going to do for the next forty-two years?" and have been overwhelmed by the huge volume of information that is available about different employment options for graduates, then don't worry, you are not alone.

A good first step would be to go and see your university careers service – every university in the UK has one – and find out about the help they can offer. Most provide a wealth of reference material about individual employers and career sectors, a diary of the talks, presentations and other events coming up at your university, and personal guidance from professional careers advisers.

The sooner you can make your first visit to the careers service – or at least look at their website – the better. Beginning your careers research in your first or second year can help take the pressure off the final year and make job-hunting less of a rush at the end of your degree. It might also enable you to organise an internship or other work experience with employers during your holidays that could lead to an offer of a permanent graduate job.

If you're in the category of 'I haven't a clue what I want to do' then a useful starting point might be Prospects Planner, the 'I speak your job' machine. This computer-based system guides you through a brief exploration of your

personality, abilities and aspirations before recommending possible career areas that may be worth exploring.

You might also want to seek help from a careers adviser, either through a booked appointment or on a drop-in 'quick query' basis. An introductory chat of ten or fifteen minutes will enable an adviser to identify your particular needs and it could be the first of several conversations.

At this stage, having thought about your abilities, interests and strengths you might only be able to express your career aims in fairly loose terms 'I'm looking for a role that involves communication and team working'. But by talking to a careers adviser and attending events at the careers service you can begin to identify which sectors are worth researching further, whether it be deep sea fishing, joining the Army or becoming a chartered accountant.

Careers advisers will not tell you which employers to apply to, but they will guide you through decision-making and give you an effective 'to-do' list to take you to the next step of the job-hunting process. If an adviser is doing their job well, they won't recommend individual organisations but they'll suggest a number of opportunities in a given area to consider. Your Careers Service is funded by your University, so the advice and information you receive there will be impartial and given in your best interests,

BRIGHT · SAVVY
FAIR · LIVELY
BRAVE · CURIOUS

HUNGRY

Not everyone will share our determination and hunger for success, but if you do, and you want to work with a leading business that will satisfy your hunger with commitments and action, you should think seriously about joining forces with us.

OPEN · FRESH
KEEN · CREATIVE
RESILIENT · TRUE

If you are hungry for success
and want to find out more visit
www.sainsburys.co.uk/graduates

Sainsbury's
Try something new tod

unlike some commercial agencies who profit by being paid commission by selected employers.

A key part of a careers adviser's role is confirming your interests and weighing up whether the career plans that you are considering sound sensible and achievable. If so, then the adviser will aid and abet you to achieve your ambition but if, on the other hand, you have some over-ambitious aims to become a High Court judge after leaving university or captain the QE2 then the careers adviser may well try to steer you towards a more appropriate path to reach your goals in the longer term.

Once you have established the kind of employers that you wish to pursue, there are a number of different ways to investigate what opportunities are available. If you look online, your university careers service website and Prospects – prospects.ac.uk – provide in-depth information on most careers destinations, as well as the latest vacancy details for specific organisations. Every major employer has a recruitment section on their own website which should provide up-to-date information on their openings for graduates. This research is an essential step towards drawing up a short-list of the employers that you might try and meet in person before making your job applications.

Many of the biggest graduate recruiters tour the UK each autumn. They typically book a room in a local hotel or within a university department, offer a glass of warm white wine with a chicken drumstick and present why their organisation is the best to join. But more importantly, these events give you the chance to meet and quiz employers in person and talk directly to recent recruits to find out whether the jobs really live up to all the glossy marketing. It's a great opportunity to ask them things like: what time they got home from work each day last week, how quickly their salary is progressing and what's the biggest pressure they've had to deal with in their job.

Before you go along to a presentation, it's a good idea to do your homework on the employer, if only to confirm that it's really worth giving up an evening to see them at all. Once you are there and in conversation with their recruitment staff, there's a chance that they may remember you if you come across as knowledgeable and enthusiastic about their organisation. They might

just scribble your name on the back of a napkin in the hope of finding your application a week or so later. It's probably best not to turn up with your CV – it looks a little desperate – but applying two or three days after the event, mentioning in your covering letter the excellent presentation and the representatives you met can give your application a more personal touch.

Look out too for events run by your careers service, such as careers fairs where you have the chance to see a number of different organisations under the same roof. Again these are a good way to meet with employers, look them in the eye and quiz them before you make your applications. You should be able to find out exactly what they're looking for, how and when to apply, and have a discussion with their recruitment staff. In some cases this may help you make a stronger, more-tailored application. By addressing it 'Dear Fred, It was good to have met you yesterday at the Cambridge Careers Fair' could give you an edge on the impersonal approaches that recruiters receive.

Once you've had the opportunity to research the employers that interest you and have shortlisted the organisations you want to pursue, it is important to check the timings for their application and selection process. Many employers do have a final closing date, but you may well be better off applying shortly after a company's campus presentation because this shows your enthusiasm for their graduate opportunities and it helps spread the time you spend filling in forms over the term. Be warned that the first application you make could take up to six hours to complete, although subsequent forms should be easier and quicker.

The other advantage of approaching companies on a 'drip feed' basis is that if your early applications start to go wrong and you're getting a series of rejections, it allows you to make changes to your later applications. There is no 'right' number of applications to attempt but you're always better off making fewer, high quality, well-targeted applications rather than trying to fill in hundreds. For an able applicant, with the right criteria, eight to a dozen applications should result in a job offer or two.

When you are filling in application forms remember that employers often have a very ambitious shopping list for what they're looking for in an 'ideal applicant' – rarely will they actually recruit someone who ticks all these boxes. So if you look at an employer's requirements, don't be put off if you match some but not all of their criteria. Obviously if it's a fundamental thing such as not being able to speak fluent Mandarin then you shouldn't continue with your application. But if it's something like presentation skills, then that's the kind of thing you may be able to persuade a prospective employer you can learn once you start work.

Much of the application process is about providing evidence of the skills you've developed and the way you've applied them during your time at university. Talking things through with a careers adviser can help you figure out how best to match the experiences you've had with the key attributes that recruiters say they are looking for. For example, if you've been captain of the netball team, should you use this as an example of leadership skills or competitiveness or even your planning and organisational skills. It can be quite hard to make sure you show off your abilities and achievements in the most appropriate way.

If your application is successful and you are invited for an interview, then the good news is that the odds on landing an eventual job offer improve very considerably – employers do not waste time meeting people who are 'no-hopers'. But many students do get turned down at interview by not showing enough interest and commitment to the organisation. The main support that your careers service can provide at this stage is either interview practise sessions or feedback from other students who have been through the process already.

The largest employers recruiting for the largest number of vacancies do still visit a number of universities to conduct their first interviews on campus but most will invite students to their offices or a regional centre or will opt for a structured telephone interview instead.

Assuming that you make it through the interview, employers may well have a final selection round in the form of a full day assessment centre at their head office. This can include further interviews, tests and group exercises. It can be hard to make specific

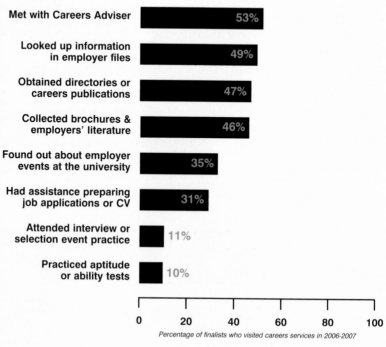

Careers Service Facilities used in 2006-7

Met with Careers Adviser	53%
Looked up information in employer files	49%
Obtained directories or careers publications	47%
Collected brochures & employers' literature	46%
Found out about employer events at the university	35%
Had assistance preparing job applications or CV	31%
Attended interview or selection event practice	11%
Practiced aptitude or ability tests	10%

0   20   40   60   80   100

Percentage of finalists who visited careers services in 2006-2007

Source **The UK Graduate Careers Survey 2007**, High Fliers Research Ltd. 17,170 final year students who left university in the summer of 2007 were asked about the facilities that they'd used at their local university careers service during 2006-2007.

Discover the real BT

Everyone knows BT, but you might not know all the things we're up to these days. From pioneering wi-fi communications and helping to count the Big Brother eviction votes to creating Vision, our new home entertainment service. We are changing the way people communicate in nearly 200 countries around the world.

Our graduates tell us that these are just some of the reasons they joined BT:

- The strength of our graduate programme
- The tailored support and training
- The real responsibility they receive from day one
- The chance to work on cutting-edge technology
- Our commitment to sustainability and CSR

Find out more about what you could be involved in as a graduate at bt.com/grads

We've combined the appeal of TV with the interactivity of Broadband to create the V-box. With the ability to store up to 80 hours of content, customers can now watch what they want when they want.

BT

Bringing it all together

INVESTOR IN PEOPLE

BT is an equal opportunity employer

preparations for these but there are a number of online tests you can try out and DVDs from AGCAS which offer useful guidance. Assessment centres can be quite scary, especially if it's the first one you've attended, but remember that although you are competing with everyone else in the room, it's not like The Apprentice. All eight candidates might well get a job offer, so you don't necessarily need to outshine the others to get a place.

Don't forget that these events are also a chance for you to weigh up the employer for a final time too. At every good assessment centre, there'll be ample scope for applicants to ask interviewers questions and meet with recent graduates over a cup of coffee.

When you receive an offer of employment, then you should congratulate yourself, you've achieved a major trophy. Check it over carefully – make sure the salary is correct, that the start date is reasonable and that there are no terms and conditions that worry you. When you're happy with the offer, the first thing you should do is acknowledge you've received it, thank the employer and let them know how chuffed you are

to have got it. Then you can weigh up when you'll be able to make a decision.

Don't be perturbed by employers who want a quick answer. If you feel you're being put under undue pressure to accept an offer, just stop and think 'why are they doing this, is this really the employer you want to work for if they treat you like this?'. You can also let the careers service know of your situation – you might be one of a dozen students at your institution who've got a similar story and careers advisers may be able to speak directly to the employer on your behalf.

A practical problem at this stage is that the other employers you've applied to may not have progressed your application as quickly, so you won't know for some time whether you'll get any additional offers. If you face that situation, try and be as open and honest as you can with the employer that has made you an offer already. By being up front with them and saying 'I really want to join your organisation, but it is a major decision and it's a decision that I want to get right' you should be able to buy yourself some extra time.

Once you have accepted an offer with one

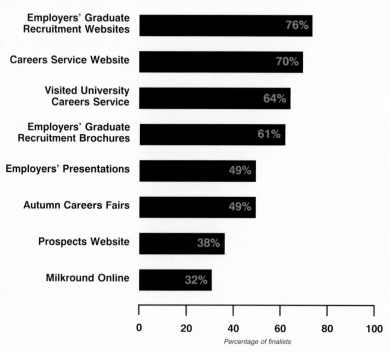

Recruitment Promotions used in 2006-7

Employers' Graduate Recruitment Websites	76%
Careers Service Website	70%
Visited University Careers Service	64%
Employers' Graduate Recruitment Brochures	61%
Employers' Presentations	49%
Autumn Careers Fairs	49%
Prospects Website	38%
Milkround Online	32%

Percentage of finalists

Source **The UK Graduate Careers Survey 2007**, High Fliers Research Ltd. 17,170 final year students who left university in the summer of 2007 were asked about the recruitment promotions that they'd used or taken part in during 2006-2007.

Moment of inspiration
27th August 2005. Accra.

Our groundbreaking microbanking scheme turns a traditional Ghanian money collector into a venture capitalist

Will Derban, Financial Inclusion Manager, spotted something life-changing in a market in Accra: the potential to alleviate poverty by connecting modern finance with one of Africa's oldest forms of banking – Susu collection. Microbanking in Ghana – targeting those whose individual income is too small for 'high street' banking – has now given nearly half a million market traders greater financial security plus the money to build their businesses. It's also given us a £multi-million business stream.

Ideas like Will's don't just make us a more successful bank. They make us a more inspiring place to work. If you'd like to add to them, visit www.inspiredbybarclays.com

Graduate Careers in Business Banking, Retail Banking, Barclaycard, Tax, Treasury, Finance, IT, HR, Marketing and Chief Administration Office

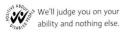

BARCLAYS
Now there's a thought

employer, tell all other employers you have applied to that you wish to withdraw your application.

If after all your applications, interviews and selection events you don't manage to secure an offer, the important thing is not to lose heart. You are certainly still employable and there will be plenty of employers who'd be keen to hear from you. Fortunately the graduate recruitment cycle in the UK is virtually a round-the-year exercise now and many small or middle-sized companies aren't driven by academic years at all – they recruit people as they need them and so have vacancies occurring at all sorts of different times.

If you find yourself job hunting directly after final exams, there are more and more summer fairs taking place across the UK. There's a major event held in London each year but many individual universities now hold their own locally too. Employers realise that increasing numbers of students delay their career research until after they've completed their studies – they'd rather get their 2.1 first and devote their time in their final year to studying rather than sitting on trains to and from job interviews.

There is no such thing as being 'too late to apply' but for a number of sectors, recruitment does follow a prescribed timetable and if you have your heart set on joining one of these areas, you'll probably need to think about taking a year out. That may not be a bad plan, particularly if you can use the year sensibly to build up your CV and acquire new expertise like computing skills or a foreign language. By dividing your year into three or four parts you could do a short-term dull but well-paid job to help pay for things, a few months voluntary work and then try for a graduate-level internship. Putting these experiences together will help make you much more marketable and potential employers will be getting a better product than if they'd recruited you straight from university.

Postgraduate study could be part of your plan too. Some students choose to do so because of the intellectual challenge and their interest in the subject. Others opt for further study because they haven't got their careers sorted out and it can be a good way of putting things on the backburner for a year or two – a nice, if somewhat expensive, delaying tactic. And then there are a few career areas that are only open to those with specific postgraduate qualifications such as law or medicine. More study can be a double-edged sword, though, because many graduates with higher qualifications do end up applying for jobs that are open to those with only a first degree, leaving them wondering why they bothered doing an extra course at all.

And, once you've sorted out your future, do stay in touch with your Careers Service, let them know what you're doing, provide some feedback on your job along with tips and advice to fellow students in the years behind you – they'll appreciate it.

THE TIMES

TOP 100

GRADUATE EMPLOYERS

Leading Destinations for 2007 Graduates

		% who wanted to work in sector			% who wanted to work in sector
1.	Media	13.4	11. Human Resources		6.9
2.	Teaching	12.7	12. Sales		5.7
3.	Investment Banking	12.4	13. General Management		5.4
4.	Marketing	11.8	14. Finance		5.0
5.	Accountancy	11.1	15. Retailing		4.6
6.	Consulting	10.2	16. IT		4.4
7.	Charity or Voluntary Work	9.5	17. Buying or Purchasing		2.9
8.	Research & Development	9.5	18. Armed Forces		2.8
9.	Law	9.2	19. Property		2.6
10.	Engineering	8.1	20. Police		2.5

Source **The UK Graduate Careers Survey 2007**, High Fliers Research Ltd. 17,170 final year students who left university in the summer of 2007 were asked which sectors they had applied to or planned to apply to for a graduate job.

Some think
training.

We think
investment.

Training is something that people *do* to graduate trainees when they want them earning their keep as fast as possible. *Learning*, on the other hand, is not a destination, but a journey: it's an attitude that sees opportunities for growth and development in every new experience. Learning is an investment you embrace as if your future depended on it – because it does. About 80% of our current revenue comes from business areas that didn't exist twenty years ago. We are very keen to prepare our people for the new, the unexpected and the unusual. Where can you learn more? See our website.

www.credit-suisse.com/careers

Thinking New Perspectives.

CREDIT SUISSE

Stay

You've already proved yourself at university – whether you've finished it yet or not. Now it's time to turn academic excellence few can match into career success that few will emulate. Visit www.mars.com/ultimategrads

a cut
above.

with **Beef**

HEALTHY HAPPY DOG FOR LIFE

Pedigree

THE TIMES — TOP 100 GRADUATE EMPLOYERS — 1997-1998

THE TIMES — TOP 100 GRADUATE EMPLOYERS — 1998-1999

THE TIMES — TOP 100 GRADUATE EMPLOYERS — 1999-2000

THE TIMES — TOP 100 GRADUATE EMPLOYERS — 2000-2001

THE TIMES — TOP 100 GRADUATE EMPLOYERS — 2001-2002

THE TIMES — TOP 100 GRADUATE EMPLOYERS — 2002-2003

THE TIMES — TOP 100 GRADUATE EMPLOYERS — 2003-2004

THE TIMES — TOP 100 GRADUATE EMPLOYERS — 2004-2005

THE TIMES — TOP 100 GRADUATE EMPLOYERS — 2005-2006

THE TIMES — TOP 100 GRADUATE EMPLOYERS — 2006-2007

THE TIMES — TOP 100 GRADUATE EMPLOYERS — 2007-2008

Ten Years of Researching Britain's Top Employers

by Martin Birchall
Managing Director, High Fliers Research

It is now a decade since the original edition of *The Times Top 100 Graduate Employers* league table was produced in 1997, revealing for the first time which organisations the UK's top undergraduates aspired to work for after their studies.

It turned out to be quite a year – Tony Blair swept into Government, ending 18 years of Conservative rule, Katrina and the Waves won the Eurovision Song Contest for the UK and Hong Kong was returned to China. Bill Clinton began his second term as President of the United States, Diana Princess of Wales was killed in a car crash in Paris, and a previously-unknown web domain 'Google' was registered in California.

For new graduates fresh out of university, 1997 was a great time to be job hunting. Vacancies were up by almost a fifth, the largest increase since the late 1980s and salaries continued to rise well above the rate of inflation. Final year students participating in *The UK Graduate Careers Survey 1997* – the annual survey of finalists' career aspirations and expectations conducted by High Fliers Research – voted Marks & Spencer the year's top graduate employer and more finalists applied for jobs in engineering than any other area.

It is interesting to compare the results of that survey with the similar research carried out with the 'Class of 2007' earlier this year. A decade ago more than half of the top twenty employers

that students thought offered the best opportunities for graduates were manufacturing or industrial companies. By contrast, just four of the organisations in this year's top twenty actually make anything – the list is dominated instead by accounting & professional services firms, high street banks and public sector employers. Investment banks received the largest number of graduate applications.

This year, typical salaries at a *Top 100* graduate employer are £25,500, an impressive 65% higher than the starting rates for graduates ten years ago. The average then was £15,500 and fewer than 30 employers in the UK offered new recruits packages of £20,000 or more.

Less than one in eight finalists used the internet in 1997 to research their career options but record numbers supported local university careers fairs. During the 2006-2007 recruitment season, although over three-quarters of students relied on employers' websites as one of their primary sources of graduate job information, attendances at campus careers events such as recruitment presentations remained strong.

Only four organisations have made it to number one since *The Times Top 100 Graduate Employers* began. Accenture (originally known as Andersen Consulting, the consulting arm of accounting firm Arthur Andersen) stormed to the top spot in 1998 and remained there for five consecutive years. Their reign heralded a huge

Fancy a challenge?

Unilever Graduate Leadership Programme

At Unilever we're responsible for producing some of the world's most popular food, home and personal care brands. So if you've got a big appetite for success, you'll find our range of opportunities a truly mouth watering prospect.

Whether you join us in **Supply Chain, Marketing, Customer Development, Innovation & Technology Management, Financial Management** or **Information Technology** you'll benefit from world-class training; you'll gain a range of experience from up to four work placements; and you'll develop all the skills you need to become a future business leader.

So think: could you get stuck into the challenge of making well-loved brands like Lynx, Dove, Walls, Flora, Persil and Ben and Jerry's even more popular? Could you hold your own with some of the most talented, creative and inspirational people in the industry? If so, you could soon be looking forward to a exciting career. Hungry for more? Visit www.unilever.co.uk/careers

Could it be
Unilever

surge in popularity for careers in consulting and at its peak in 2001 almost one in six university graduates applied for jobs in the sector. In the year before the firm changed its name, Andersen Consulting astutely introduced a new graduate package that included a £28,500 starting salary (a sky-high figure for graduates in 2000) and a much talked-about £10,000 bonus, helping to assure the firm's popularity, irrespective of its corporate branding.

In 2003, after two dismal years in graduate recruitment when vacancies for university-leavers dropped by more than a fifth following the terrorist attacks of 11th September 2001, the Civil Service was named Britain's leading graduate employer. A year later it was displaced by PricewaterhouseCoopers, the accounting and professional services firm formed from the merger of Price Waterhouse and Coopers & Lybrand in 1998. At the time, the firm was the largest private-sector recruiter of graduates, hiring over 1,000 trainees annually.

PricewaterhouseCoopers has now stayed at number one for four years running, increasing its share of the student vote from 5 per cent in 2004 to more than 10 per cent in 2007, despite stiff competition from its close rivals Deloitte and KPMG. This period represents a remarkable renaissance for the entire accounting sector. Whereas a decade ago, a career in accountancy was widely regarded as a safe, traditional employment choice and the firms themselves were often derided as being 'dull', 'boring' 'bean-counters', today's profession is viewed in a very different light. The training required to become a

chartered accountant is seen as a prized business qualification and the sector's leading employers are regularly described as 'prestigious', 'dynamic' and 'international' by undergraduates.

Accountancy's transformation is underlined by the fact that just 7 per cent of final year students opted for one of the top six accounting firms in *Top 100* of 1997, compared with the 22 per cent of votes polled by the 'Big Four' firms in this year's list.

A total of 174 different organisations have now appeared within *The Times Top 100 Graduate Employers* since its inception. Just twenty-four of these have made it into the rankings every year since 1997. The most consistent performers have been Accenture and the Civil Service – both of which have never been lower than 8th place in the league table. Procter & Gamble has also had a formidable record, appearing in every top ten until 2007, and Ernst & Young, KPMG, IBM and Unilever have each remained within the top quarter of the list throughout.

Arthur Andersen, the now defunct accounting firm, was actually the most consistently ranked employer in the history of the *Top 100*, achieving either 2nd or 3rd place every year between 1997 and the firm's demise in 2002. Pricewaterhouse-Coopers is the only other employer to have appeared within the top three in each of the years in which it has been listed in the *Top 100*.

Not all employers have been so successful. Chemical company ICI, ranked in 5th place in 1997, dropped out of the *Top 100* altogether in 2001 but has made three reappearances since.

THE TIMES
TOP 100
GRADUATE EMPLOYERS

Movers & Shakers in the Top 100

Highest New Entries		Highest Climbing Employers	
1998	**Microsoft** (38th)	1998	**JPMorgan** (up 8 places)
1999	**Pfizer** (31st)	1999	**Schlumberger** (up 13 places)
2000	**Morgan Stanley** (34th)	2000	**Capital One** (up 32 places)
2001	**Marconi** (36th)	2001	**European Commission** (up 36 places)
2002	**Guinness UDV** (44th)	2002	**WPP** (up 36 places)
2003	**ASDA** (40th)	2003	**Rolls-Royce** (up 37 places)
2004	**Baker & McKenzie** (61st)	2004	**JPMorgan** (up 29 places)
2005	**Penguin** (70th)	2005	**Teach First** (up 22 places)
2006	**Fujitsu** (81st)	2006	**Google** (up 32 places)
2007	**BDO Stoy Hayward** (74th)	2007	**Pfizer** (up 30 places)

Source **The UK Graduate Careers Survey 1997-2006**, High Fliers Research Ltd, based on interviews with 153,179 students.

Be surprised.
Learn something new.
Find direction.

Think about
Barclays Capital.

Graduate and Intern Opportunities

BARCLAYS CAPITAL

British Airways fell over eighty places in the years between 1999 and 2004 and high street chemist Boots has slumped from 6th in 1998 to 75th in this year's rankings.

Ford – which was once rated as high as 11th – fell out of the list in 2006 after cancelling its graduate recruitment two years previously. And the Ministry of Defence, which despite reaching 35th place for its engineering & science graduate scheme in 2003, has since taken such a low-key approach to its campus marketing that it was unranked in the latest league table.

Twenty-eight employers including well-known names such as Nokia, Philips, the Home Office, Abbey, Coca-Cola and British Sugar have the dubious record of having only been ranked in the *Top 100* once during the decade, before disppearing without trace. Marconi had the unusual distinction of being one of the highest-ever new entries in 36th place in 2001, only to vanish from the list entirely the following year.

One of the most spectacular ascendancies within the *Top 100* has been the rise and rise of Aldi which joined the list in 65th place in 2002 and is now ranked 9th in the 2007 league table. Its eye-catching remuneration package (currently £39,000 plus an Audi A4 car for new graduates joining in 2008) coupled with the lofty job title of 'deputy area manager' for its new recruits and the promise of rapid career progression for those who thrive at the company, have really captured the imagination of increasing numbers of student job hunters.

And Teach First – the innovative scheme which recruits graduates to work in teaching for two years after university before they embark on careers in other areas – has been another runaway success in the rankings. After appearing in the *The Times Top 100 Graduate Employers* as a new entry in 63rd place in 2003, the scheme is currently ranked 14th and seems likely to rise further still in future.

THE TIMES TOP 100 GRADUATE EMPLOYERS

Winners & Losers in the Top 100

Most Consistent Employers 1997-2007

	Highest Ranking	Lowest Ranking
Arthur Andersen*	2nd (1998-2001)	3rd (1997, 2002)
PricewaterhouseCoopers*	1st (2004-2007)	3rd (1999-2001, 2003)
Accenture (formerly Andersen Consulting)	1st (1998-2002)	8th (2006)
Civil Service	1st (2003)	8th (1997)
Ernst & Young	11th (2007)	21st (1998)
IBM	12th (1997)	25th (1998)
Procter & Gamble	2nd (1997)	15th (2007)
Army	4th (2003)	18th (2007)
GlaxoSmithKline	11th (2000)	26th (1998)
KPMG	3rd (2006-2007)	20th (1997)
Unilever	6th (1997)	23rd (2007)
Clifford Chance	26th (2002)	45th (2007)

Employer did not feature in the Top 100 every year between 1997 and 2007

Employers Falling Furthest 1997-2007

	Highest Ranking	Lowest Ranking
ICI	5th (1997)	Not ranked (2001, 2004, 2006-2007)
British Airways	6th (1999)	87th (2004)
Boots	6th (1998)	75th (2007)
Ford	11th (1999)	Not ranked (2006-2007)
Ministry of Defence	35th (2003)	Not ranked (2007)
Logica	39th (1999)	Not ranked (2003-2007)
GKN	40th (1999)	Not ranked (2002-2007)
QinetiQ	43rd (2001)	Not ranked (2007)
Capital One	44th (2001)	Not ranked (2003-2007)
Nestlé	46th (1999)	Not ranked (2005-2007)
Nortel	47th (1998)	Not ranked (2003-2007)

Source **The UK Graduate Careers Survey 1997-2006**, High Fliers Research Ltd, based on interviews with 153,179 students.

THE TIMES TOP 100 GRADUATE EMPLOYERS

Top 10 Graduate Employers 1997-2006

1997
1. Marks & Spencer
2. Procter & Gamble
3. Arthur Andersen
4. Andersen Consulting (now Accenture)
5. ICI
6. Unilever
7. BP
8. Civil Service
9. Shell
10. Boots

1998
1. Andersen Consulting (now Accenture)
2. Arthur Andersen
3. Procter & Gamble
4. Marks & Spencer
5. Civil Service
6. Boots
7. Unilever
8. KPMG
9. Price Waterhouse
10. British Airways

1999
1. Andersen Consulting (now Accenture)
2. Arthur Andersen
3. PricewaterhouseCoopers
4. Procter & Gamble
5. Civil Service
6. British Airways
7. Marks & Spencer
8. KPMG
9. Unilever
10. Boots

2000
1. Andersen Consulting (now Accenture)
2. Arthur Andersen
3. PricewaterhouseCoopers
4. Procter & Gamble
5. KPMG
6. Civil Service
7. Army
8. Unilever
9. Mars
10. BBC

2001
1. Accenture
2. Arthur Andersen
3. PricewaterhouseCoopers
4. Procter & Gamble
5. Goldman Sachs
6. Civil Service
7. KPMG
8. Unilever
9. Army
10. Mars

2002
1. Accenture
2. PricewaterhouseCoopers
3. Andersen (formerly Arthur Andersen)
4. Civil Service
5. Army
6. KPMG
7. Unilever
8. Procter & Gamble
9. Goldman Sachs
10. Mars

2003
1. Civil Service
2. Accenture
3. PricewaterhouseCoopers
4. Army
5. KPMG
6. HSBC
7. BBC
8. Procter & Gamble
9. NHS
10. Deloitte & Touche (now Deloitte)

2004
1. PricewaterhouseCoopers
2. Civil Service
3. Accenture
4. KPMG
5. NHS
6. BBC
7. Army
8. Procter & Gamble
9. HSBC
10. Deloitte

2005
1. PricewaterhouseCoopers
2. Civil Service
3. Accenture
4. KPMG
5. BBC
6. Deloitte
7. NHS
8. HSBC
9. Goldman Sachs
10. Procter & Gamble

2006
1. PricewaterhouseCoopers
2. Deloitte
3. KPMG
4. Civil Service
5. BBC
6. NHS
7. HSBC
8. Accenture
9. Procter & Gamble
10. Goldman Sachs

Source **The UK Graduate Careers Survey 1997-2006**, High Fliers Research Ltd, based on interviews with 153,179 students.

At Faber Maunsell we balance progress and sustainability, invention and practicality, global challenges and local needs, work and life, your dreams and our business success.

Discover more at
www.fabermaunsell.com

FABER MAUNSELL | AECOM

dreams | success

WHAT IF PEOPLE ASKED HOW YOU WERE AND REALLY WANTED TO KNOW?

ARE YOU SURE YOU'RE OK, MIKE?

BDO Stoy Hayward is the UK's fastest growing major accountancy firm and part of one of the world's leading international networks, with more than 600 offices in over 100 countries. It's an exciting time to join us with opportunities to grow with our success. But our growth alone is not what makes us special. It's the open and supportive culture of our firm that means we have been voted Accountancy Age's Employer of the Year and we have been voted as one of the Top 50 places Where Women Want To Work by the Times.
Apply online at www.bdo.co.uk/careers

YOU'LL NOTICE THE DIFFERENCE

Global Firm of the Year 2006
Employer of the Year 2005

BDO Stoy Hayward
Chartered Accountants

Index

	Accountancy	Consulting	Engineering	Finance	General Management	Human Resources	Investment Banking	IT	Law	Logistics	Manufacturing	Marketing	Media	Purchasing	Research & Development	Retailing	Sales	Other
ABN AMRO							•	•										
Accenture		•						•										
Addleshaw Goddard									•									
Aldi																•		
Allen & Overy									•									
Arcadia			•		•							•			•			
Army			•	•	•			•		•								
ASDA				•	•			•		•						•	•	
AstraZeneca			•	•				•			•			•	•			
Atkins		•	•															
BAE Systems			•	•	•			•			•			•	•			•
Baker & McKenzie									•									
Bank of America							•	•										
Barclays Bank	•		•	•	•			•			•					•	•	
Barclays Capital	•	•	•	•			•											
BDO Stoy Hayward	•	•	•					•										
Bloomberg			•					•					•		•			•
BP	•		•	•	•			•						•			•	
BT	•		•	•	•			•				•	•	•	•		•	
Cadbury Schweppes		•	•		•					•	•	•		•	•			•
Cancer Research UK	•		•		•	•		•	•				•	•		•		
Capgemini		•						•										
Citi					•		•	•										
Civil Service Fast Stream					•			•										
Clifford Chance									•									
Co-operative Group				•	•													
Corus			•	•		•					•	•		•	•			
Credit Suisse				•			•	•										
Deloitte	•	•		•				•										
Deutsche Bank	•			•	•		•	•	•									
DLA Piper									•									
Ernst & Young	•	•		•				•										
Eversheds									•									
ExxonMobil	•		•	•	•			•			•					•	•	
Faber Maunsell		•	•															
Financial Services Authority			•															
Freshfields Bruckhaus Deringer									•									
Fujitsu	•	•		•				•			•			•				•
GCHQ	•							•						•	•			
GE	•		•	•	•			•			•	•					•	
GlaxoSmithKline	•		•	•				•						•	•			•
Goldman Sachs	•			•	•		•	•										

	Accountancy	Consulting	Engineering	Finance	General Management	Human Resources	Investment Banking	IT	Law	Logistics	Manufacturing	Marketing	Media	Purchasing	Research & Development	Retailing	Sales	Other
Google				●				●				●		●		●		
HBOS	●			●	●	●	●	●	●			●				●	●	
HSBC	●			●	●	●	●	●	●			●				●	●	
IBM	●	●		●				●							●			
John Lewis																●		
JPMorgan				●			●	●										
KPMG	●			●	●							●					●	
L'Oréal				●								●					●	
Linklaters									●									
Lloyds TSB	●			●	●	●		●				●				●	●	
Lovells									●									
Maersk				●	●	●												
Marks & Spencer						●		●						●		●		
Mars			●	●	●							●		●			●	
McDonald's Restaurants				●										●				
McKinsey & Company		●																
Mercer		●	●															
Merrill Lynch					●		●							●				
Metropolitan Police																		●
MI5 – The Security Service			●	●		●		●										
Microsoft								●				●					●	
Morgan Stanley							●	●										
NGDP for Local Government					●													
NHS					●	●												
npower			●	●	●			●										
Oxfam	●				●	●		●				●	●		●	●		
Penguin	●			●					●			●	●			●	●	
Police HPDS																		●
PricewaterhouseCoopers	●	●							●									
Procter & Gamble	●		●	●	●	●		●			●	●		●	●			
Reuters	●		●					●					●					
Rolls-Royce			●	●		●				●	●			●				
Royal Bank of Scotland Group	●			●		●	●	●				●					●	
Sainsbury's				●		●						●		●		●		
Shell			●	●				●									●	
Slaughter and May									●									
Teach First	●	●	●	●	●	●	●	●	●	●	●	●	●	●	●	●	●	
Tesco	●	●	●	●		●		●	●	●	●	●		●	●	●	●	
Transport for London	●		●	●	●	●		●				●						
UBS				●		●	●	●									●	
Unilever			●	●							●	●		●	●		●	
WPP Group												●	●					

ABN·AMRO

Vacancies for around
150 graduates in 2008

- Investment Banking
- IT

Vacancies also available in Europe,
Asia and elsewhere in the world.

Starting salary for 2008
£Competitive

Universities ABN AMRO
plans to visit in 2007-8
Bristol, Cambridge, City,
Dublin, Edinburgh, Exeter,
London, Nottingham,
Oxford, Reading,
St Andrews, Warwick
Please check with your university
careers service for details of events.

Application deadline
4th November 2007

Contact Details
✉ abnamrograd08@
alexmann.com
☎ 0870 351 3704

Turn to page 224 now to request
more information about ABN AMRO.

ABN AMRO is a prominent international bank, with a history going back to 1824. They're ranked 8th in Europe and 13th in the world based on total assets, with more than 4,500 branches in 53 countries, a staff of more than 107,000 full-time equivalents and total assets of €1,054.60 billion (as at 31st March 2007).

With a relationship-based approach and client-led strategy, they create value for clients, from mass retail to high net worth individuals, and corporate and institutional organisations. A strong corporate culture is based on integrity, teamwork, respect and professionalism, which enables them to make more possible for their clients and employees alike. They believe it's a unique culture in the sector – where people are open to new ideas, aren't afraid to voice their opinions and are prepared to listen to other people's views.

Their global graduate development programme begins with six weeks' training at their exclusive academy in Amsterdam. Graduates then complete a series of rotational placements in sales and trading, banking, group risk management, technology, or asset management. Graduates receive extensive support and development opportunities with the chance to study for professional qualifications where appropriate.

They're looking for highly ambitious, enthusiastic graduates of the highest academic calibre. Thought leaders who have the practical skills to get things done. People with the confidence, initiative and team spirit to build strong relationships with clients and colleagues.

In London ABN AMRO also runs a summer internship programme which lasts for ten to twelve weeks and commences in early July 2008.

At ABN AMRO we look for people who can think laterally and act decisively to develop effective solutions for our clients. This brainteaser will get you thinking.

Two American racing drivers were rivals to become CEO of a major car firm owned by a businessman in Chicago. The businessman didn't like either man, so came up with a plan – a race to decide who'd take over the firm. Both men had to drive from New York to Chicago, and the one whose car arrived last in Chicago would become CEO. The racers realised this could take a long time, so they went to a wise man and explained the situation. The wise man spoke four words and the two drivers left his office prepared to race. What did the wise man say?

INDIVIDUAL IN OUR THINKING,
GLOBAL IN OUR OUTLOOK.

Global graduate opportunities in corporate and investment banking

Our graduate development programme offers opportunities across Europe, North America and Asia Pacific. Wherever you join us you'll enjoy the scope to think innovatively, take early responsibility and tackle a variety of complex challenges. A place where you'll appreciate a culture that values your work/life balance as much as your skills.

For the answer, as well as details of our global graduate development programme, go to
www.graduate.abnamro.com

Making more possible

accenture
High performance. Delivered.

**Vacancies for around
500 graduates in 2008**

■ Consulting

■ IT

**Starting salary for 2008
£31,000**
Plus £10,000 bonus.

**Universities Accenture
plans to visit in 2007-8**
Aston, Bath, Birmingham,
Bristol, Cambridge,
Durham, Edinburgh,
Glasgow, Leeds, London,
Loughborough, Manchester,
Newcastle, Nottingham,
Oxford, Sheffield,
St Andrews, Warwick
Please check with your university
careers service for details of events.

Application deadline
Year-round recruitment

Contact Details
✉ ukgraduates@accenture.com
☎ 0500 100 189
Turn to page 224 now to request
more information about Accenture.

With over 158,000 people working in 49 countries, Accenture is one of the world's leading management consulting, technology services and outsourcing organisations and their work invariably involves the application of information technology to business challenges.

Accenture believe that they offer great opportunities for graduates, partly because of the work they do, and partly because learning and personal development are so high on their agenda. Graduates control their own development and promotion is based entirely on the skills they acquire and the contribution they make, whilst flexible working programmes allow them to manage their schedule to suit them.

Graduate joiners at Accenture will build core business, technology and industry expertise, helping to deliver world-class solutions that enable their clients to become high-performance businesses. They also actively encourage people to get involved in community and charitable activities that make a real difference to communities across the UK and around the world.

Accenture look for people with more than just excellent academics. They need individuals who are passionate about something outside their studies, who have some work experience and a strong interest in business and technology. For graduates who meet the above criteria, expect to achieve a 2:1 degree and have 320 UCAS points or equivalent, they can offer a truly rounded career.

They also have a number of schemes and placements that are designed to give an insider's view of the world of Accenture. Find out more at accenture.com/ukschemes

Tackling complicated situations with ingenuity.
Just another day at the office for a Tiger.

Accenture knows the importance of creating the right environment for success. We're one of the world's leading management consulting, technology services and outsourcing companies and we want talented people who are looking for a challenge. We offer unrivalled training and you'll be able to develop your skills faster here than almost anywhere else. Join our global team and you'll be delivering the innovation that helps our clients become high-performance businesses.

Graduate Careers in Consulting

Almost everything we do involves the application of IT to business challenges. But that's not to say you have to be a computer genius to get on here (although we certainly wouldn't hold it against you). If you're genuinely interested in business and technology, expect to achieve a 2:1 degree and have 320 UCAS points or equivalent, we can offer you a truly rounded career.

As well as doing interesting, challenging work with exceptional people, and using the latest technology, you'll be rewarded well with a salary of £31,000 and an additional £10,000 bonus.

We also encourage you to get involved in charitable activities that make a real difference to communities throughout the world. For people with the right intelligence and personal qualities, consulting is possibly the best job in the world. Discover more and apply at our website.

Accenture is committed to being an equal opportunities employer.

Visit accenture.com/ukgraduates

• Consulting • Technology • Outsourcing

accenture

High performance. Delivered.

ADDLESHAW GODDARD

www.addleshawgoddard.com/graduates

Vacancies for around
50 graduates in 2008
For training contracts starting in 2010

Law

Starting salary for 2008
£24,750-£36,000
Varies by location.

**Universities that
Addleshaw Goddard
plans to visit in 2007-8**
Birmingham, Bristol,
Cambridge, Durham, Exeter,
Leeds, Leicester, London,
Manchester, Nottingham,
Oxford, Sheffield,
St Andrews, York
Please check with your university
careers service for details of events.

Application deadline
31st July 2008

Contact Details
✉ grad@addleshawgoddard.com

Turn to page 224 now to request more
information about Addleshaw Goddard.

A leading national law firm with the capability to provide excellent service to a global client base. Ranked 15th largest law firm in the UK, Addleshaw Goddard is also ranked in The Sunday Times 100 Best Companies to work for.

The firm has four main practice areas: corporate, finance and projects, real estate and contentious and commercial.

Addleshaw Goddard are looking for graduates and undergraduates from any academic discipline who possess the motivation and commitment necessary to join a top 20 law firm and who are capable of achieving, or have achieved, at least a 2(i) degree.

During their training contract, trainees will be given the opportunity to experience a broad range of corporate and commercial work. During each six-month seat they will have regular performance reviews with their supervisor, and the on-the-job training will be supported by courses provided by the firm's in-house team and external experts.

Tuition fees are paid for both GDL and LPC courses, together with an annual maintenance grant – currently £7,000 per course for all future trainees studying the GDL or LPC in central London, and £4,500 per course for all future trainees studying elsewhere.

They have vacation schemes in their London, Leeds and Manchester offices both at Easter and Summer. For an invaluable insight into the firm and help deciding whether Addleshaw Goddard is the right destination, visit www.addleshawgoddard.com/graduates

ADDLESHAW GODDARD

EAGER

www.aldi.co.uk

Aldi is one of the world's largest privately-owned companies and, with over 7,000 stores worldwide, is recognised as a world leader in grocery retailing. They are pioneers in quality discount retailing and their unique culture and philosophy promote exceptional standards of management and deliver unrivalled value for money for their customers.

The Graduate Area Management Programme offers superb opportunities for personal and career development to exceptional graduates who can prove they have drive and focus and have a record of achievement outside academia.

An individual twelve-month training programme quickly introduces trainees to the pace and excitement of retail operations, trading, logistics and property management. Starting in-store and managing one within weeks, the programme progresses on to multi-site responsibilities, which offer trainees the broadest opportunities to develop their leadership style, commercial awareness and technical skills. As soon as Area Management trainees are ready, they'll be given a multi-million pound area with a number of stores to run as if they owned it.

Two-year secondments to Europe or further afield are a real possibility. Within five years, there's every chance of a directorship reporting to the Managing Director of a region, or the Group Buying Director.

Find out more by visiting www.aldi.co.uk and apply online. Alternatively, send a CV, quoting Times 100, with a letter demonstrating leadership potential to: Area Management Recruitment, Aldi Stores Limited, Chester High Road, Neston, Cheshire CH64 3TS.

Rocket.

Mediterranean salad ingredient
or career trajectory?

So here you are. You've always promised yourself a career where the sky's the limit. Where the possibilities are endless. No endless 9 to 5s in a career cul-de-sac – wondering exactly when it was that your 'get-up-and-go' had got up and gone. The Aldi Graduate Area Manager Training Programme could have been purpose-built to keep this bleak future at bay. It rewards enterprise, spirit and drive with a rapid rise through the ranks.

From day one, the pace is fast, but never frenetic. You'll start at the grass roots and you'll learn everyone's job by doing it yourself. From stacking shelves to working the tills. During this time, you'll sharpen your instincts for what motivates your team. You'll learn how to lead from the front and, crucially, how to drive up sales and bring down costs. In just a few short weeks, you can expect to be managing a store. Then, over the following months, you'll move into phase two of training to take on Area Management responsibilities – where you'll be given every opportunity to display your leadership skills and commercial awareness.

When this training is over, you'll have total responsibility for four to six stores, effectively managing your own multi-million pound business. It's unlikely that you'd be operating at such a heady altitude with so much authority and empowerment in any other business. But, we never said Aldi was just another ordinary business. In fact, the material rewards are extraordinary too. The starting salary is £39K plus an Audi A4, rising in annual increments to £56K after three years and includes a pension, private healthcare, life assurance and five weeks' holiday.

There are also opportunities for Area Managers to spend two years on secondment in Europe or further afield. Within five years, there is every chance of a directorship.

Dizzy heights indeed.

If you want to go further, faster, you can apply online at **www.aldi.co.uk** or send a CV together with a letter illustrating your leadership potential to: Aldi Stores Ltd, Area Management Recruitment, Chester High Road, Neston, Cheshire CH64 3TS. Please quote ref: RW01 on all applications.

Graduate
Area Manager
£39K + Audi A4
rising to
£56K + Audi A4
after 3 years
Opportunity for
directorship within
5 years

ALLEN & OVERY

www.allenovery.com/careeruk

**Vacancies for around
120 graduates in 2008**
For training contracts starting in 2010

 Law

Starting salary for 2008
£35,700

•

**Universities Allen & Overy
plans to visit in 2007-8**
Bath, Belfast, Birmingham,
Bristol, Cambridge, Cardiff,
City, Dublin, Durham,
East Anglia, Edinburgh,
Exeter, Kent, Leeds,
Leicester, Liverpool,
London, Manchester,
Newcastle, Northumbria,
Nottingham, Oxford,
Oxford Brookes, Reading,
Sheffield, Southampton,
St Andrews, Warwick, York
Please check with your university
careers service for details of events.

Application deadline
Year-round recruitment
See website for full details.

Contact Details
 graduate.recruitment
@allenovery.com
☎ 020 3088 0000
Turn to page 224 now to request more
information about Allen & Overy.

Allen & Overy is an international legal practice with 5,100 people
in 24 major centres worldwide. The practice's client list includes
many of the world's top businesses, financial institutions,
governments and private individuals.

Allen & Overy is renowned for the high quality of its banking, corporate and
international capital markets advice, but also has major strengths in dispute
resolution, tax, employment and employee benefits, real estate and private
client. Within this broad range of expertise, the practice offers a training
contract which is characterised by flexibility and choice. Training contracts
are tailored for each trainee to ensure they have the best start to their career.

Given the strength of the practice's international finance practice, trainees
spend 12 months working in banking, corporate and international capital
markets, with a contentious seat in either dispute resolution or employment.
There are also opportunities for trainees to undertake an international or client
secondment in their second year of training. By working closely with their
trainers and other colleagues, trainees develop practical experience and enjoy
a high level of early responsibility.

Vital to Allen & Overy's success is the way they approach work. Allen & Overy
people enjoy what they do and want to employ people who think in the same
way, maintaining a professional, supportive and friendly working environment.

Allen & Overy recruits 120 trainee solicitors and 100 vacation students (winter
and summer) each year. Applications from both law and non-law candidates
are welcome. At least a 2.1 degree (or equivalent) should be predicted or
achieved, with evidence of teamwork, leadership, motivation and problem-
solving as well.

Taxi drivers are required by law to ask all passengers
if they have smallpox or the plague.
☐ Law *or* ☐ Non-law?

Law and business are full of surprises. Whether you are exploring the modern implications of existing laws,
or working to find legal solutions to new situations, you'll need to be open-minded, creative and commercial.
At Allen & Overy, we are working at the forefront of today's evolving legal landscape, helping to shape and
frame the environment in which business, and life itself, is conducted.

Poxy passengers

You don't need to have studied law to become a lawyer, but business sense,
curiosity and a commitment to excellence are essential.
www.allenovery.com/careeruk

▲ Arcadia Group Limited

**Vacancies for around
250-300 graduates in 2008**

- Finance
- Human Resources
- Purchasing
- Retailing

Starting salary for 2008
£17,500-£23,000

**Universities Arcadia Group
plans to visit in 2007-8**
Please check with your university
careers service for details of events.

Application deadline
See website for full details.

Contact Details
✉ management.programmes@
arcadiagroup.co.uk

Turn to page 224 now to request more
information about Arcadia Group.

The Arcadia Group is one of the largest fashion retailers in the UK, boasting some of the most exciting and innovative brands on the high street today – Burton, Dorothy Perkins, Evans, Miss Selfridge, Outfit, Topshop, Topman and Wallis.

Arcadia offer careers that appeal to a diverse range of individuals – from graduates who have a strong numerical background to those passionate about store management, all with a passion and flair for fashion retail. Exciting career opportunities are available in retail management, buying, merchandising, distribution, finance and human resources. A limited number of placements are also available each year – please visit the website for further information.

The Arcadia Group is committed to the training and development of all of its graduates. On offer are specially designed development programmes, on the job competency based training and where appropriate support for formal qualifications, e.g. CIMA/ACCA and CIPD. With outstanding drive and commitment, graduates can achieve promotion at the earliest opportunity.

The Arcadia Group is looking for graduates with enthusiasm, commercial awareness and passion for excellent customer service coupled with a love of fashion. In return, graduates will be given early responsibility, structured training and development and the ability to make an impact on one of the most forward-thinking fashion retailers in the UK. As well as a competitive salary, successful applicants will enjoy a great benefits package including up to 25 days holiday, 25% discount on group merchandise, participation in a bonus scheme and membership of the group's pension scheme.

CAREERS
THAT SET THE TREND...

The Arcadia Group is one of the largest fashion retailers in the UK, boasting some of the most exciting and innovative brands on the high street today – Burton, Dorothy Perkins, Evans, Miss Selfridge, Outfit, Topshop, Topman and Wallis.

We are looking for bright, enthusiastic graduates with a passion and flair for fashion retail. The Arcadia Group offer exciting career opportunities in Retail Management, Buying, Merchandising, Distribution, Finance and Human Resources.

To find out more and apply online visit our website today

www.arcadiagroup.co.uk/recruitment

▲ Arcadia Group Limited

ARMY
BE THE BEST
REGULAR & TERRITORIAL

Vacancies for around 600 graduates in 2008

- Engineering
- Finance
- General Management
- Human Resources
- IT
- Logistics

Starting salary for 2008
£22,680
On appointment.

Universities the Army plans to visit in 2007-8
Please check with your university careers service for details of events.

Application deadline
Year-round recruitment

Contact Details
☎ 0845 7300 111
Turn to page 224 now to request more information about the Army.

Being an Army Officer is unlike any other job – from leading a platoon of 30 soldiers one week to organising a team on adventurous training the next. The Army engages with graduates and trains them to become some of the best leaders in the world.

As one of the most respected and technologically advanced organisations in the world, the Army can offer unrivalled training and development to graduates of all disciplines, enhancing management and leadership potential and providing the skills and self-confidence to excel in the Army and, later on, in civilian careers.

Beyond the many career-enhancing qualities in which graduates become skilled, there are many personal rewards for most Officers – they will find it incredibly satisfying to discover what they're capable of under different kinds of pressure. After just one year of training, Officers can be responsible for over 30 soldiers and several million pounds' worth of equipment.

Graduates start their Officer training at the Royal Military Academy Sandhurst where they learn all aspects of soldiering, management and leadership training. On completion, they will join their Regiment or Corps where they will undergo specialist training for their chosen occupation. Subsequently, Officers may study for Army-sponsored or vocational qualifications.

If the career development isn't enough to tempt them, perhaps some of the other aspects of being an Officer will – the Army provides a challenging career, continuous professional development, great promotional prospects, unrivalled travel and sporting opportunities and an excellent remuneration and benefits package.

GTE PIAD FRO SLVONIG PMLEBROS.

ARMY OFFICER.
HAVE YOU GOT WHAT IT TAKES?

If you enjoy a challenge and are looking for an exciting and rewarding lifestyle, the Army might be for you. Each year, the Army recruits over 600 potential Officers into Sandhurst. Some will make the Army their career, others will only stay for a few years and both will benefit from the excellent training and the lasting friendships. You can enter Sandhurst as a graduate, or if you have received financial sponsorship from the Army through university. You also have the choice with the 6th Form Scholarships, places at the Technical Defence 6th Form College at Welbeck, and a special commission just for the Gap Year without further commitment.

ARMY
BE THE BEST
REGULAR & TERRITORIAL

ASDA

www.asdagraduates.com

Vacancies for around 60 graduates in 2008

- Finance
- General Management
- Human Resources
- IT
- Logistics
- Purchasing
- Retailing
- Sales

Starting salary for 2008
£22,000

Universities that ASDA plans to visit in 2007-8
Bristol, Dundee, Edinburgh, Leeds, Loughborough, Manchester, Newcastle, Sheffield, Southampton
Please check with your university careers service for details of events.

Application deadline
Year-round recruitment

Contact Details
Turn to page 224 now to request more information about ASDA.

Voted the UK's best place to work by the Financial Times, named one of Europe's best employers by Fortune magazine, and part of Wal-Mart – the biggest name in retail – ASDA is one of the UK's fastest-growing retailers.

With over 13 million customers per week, 163,000 employees and more than 300 stores, ASDA's success is down to attitude: the fact that every person who works there is proud to be part of the team – and keen to join in wherever they're needed.

ASDA are looking for people with the potential to manage their multimillion-pound stores. But that's not all. They also have exciting opportunities in a variety of areas like Logistics, Trading, Finance, Project Management – Systems Solutions, Retail Development, HR and George. Whichever scheme graduates join, they'll be given real responsibility from an early stage and a professional, structured career path with excellent training and development opportunities.

They're looking for enthusiastic, confident types who have a real passion for retail, can take early responsibility in their stride, and aren't afraid to constructively challenge the way they work. They consider degrees in all disciplines, and are especially interested in extra-curricular experience like industrial placements or a year out. Graduates joining the Retail Management side of things will need some relevant industry experience.

On top of the salary, successful applicants will have a bonus scheme, discount card, pension, healthcare, life assurance, share plans and 24 days' holiday. They will also enjoy uncompromising support for their development, with the aim of placing them in a senior management role after five years.

DON'T BE AFRAID
TO GET YOUR HANDS
DIRTY

The spirit of joining in isn't just a nice idea, it's what fuels our business. The fact that we all get a buzz out of getting involved is key to some of our proudest achievements. It also makes ASDA a really fun place to work. So whether you want to manage a multimillion-pound store or specialise in another area like Logistics, Trading, Finance, Project Management-Systems Solutions, Retail Development, HR or GEORGE – it's time to find out what we can do for your graduate career. More than 150,000 people have already chosen to build a career with ASDA and we now have more than 300 stores across the UK. ASDA is also part of Wal-Mart, the biggest name in retail with more than 1.8 million people working across 15 countries. So find out where you can fit in at www.asdagraduates.com

JOIN IN

ASDA

AstraZeneca

Vacancies for around 15-25 graduates in 2008

- Engineering
- Finance
- IT
- Logistics
- Marketing
- Purchasing
- Research & Development

I want to be recognised

Starting salary for 2008
£25,000-£28,000

Universities AstraZeneca plans to visit in 2007-8
Please check with your university careers service for details of events.

Application deadline
Year-round recruitment
See website for full details.

Contact Details
Turn to page 224 now to request more information about AstraZeneca.

One of the world's leading pharmaceutical companies, AstraZeneca turns great ideas into innovative medicines which make real difference to peoples lives.

The company's excellent reputation and diversity of graduate opportunities make them the natural choice for candidates from a science background. However, their strengths in manufacturing and commerce mean they can also provide challenges to graduates from other disciplines. Whatever their degree subject, graduates will be excited by the quality and diversity of opportunity. Programmes are designed to progress careers through an integrated range of flexible training activities and blended learning ideas.

From day-one induction and personal mentoring to management and global leadership programmes, AstraZeneca provides the resources and support graduates need to reach their full potential; while cross-functional moves, secondments and international assignments can broaden the experience. It is a performance-based culture with competitive salaries and bonuses that are linked to overall progress. But they also believe that quality of life and quality of work go hand in hand. That's why they actively pursue opportunities for flexible working arrangements.

Core benefits include a minimum level of pension contribution and healthcare provision, and the additional range of 'rewards options' is considerable. But these are benefits that people tend to appreciate further down the line. What probably excites graduates more at this stage is the opportunity to develop their skills within a truly global business that's setting the standards in an industry rich in challenges and rewards.

Graduate opportunities, all disciplines.

It's only possible to achieve your full potential when you're given the proper support and resources. At AstraZeneca, we're committed to our graduates' success and reward people on the basis of performance.

take your ambitions forward at
ideas.astrazeneca.com
sign up for job alerts and let the opportunities come to you

AstraZeneca
life inspiring ideas

ΛTKINS

www.atkinsglobal.com/graduates

Vacancies for around
250+ graduates in 2008

███ Consulting

███ Engineering

Vacancies also available in the USA,
Asia and elsewhere in the world.

Starting salary for 2008
£Competitive

Universities that Atkins
plans to visit in 2007-8

Bath, Belfast, Birmingham,
Bristol, Cambridge,
Cardiff, Dundee, Durham,
Glasgow, Heriot-Watt,
Leeds, Liverpool,
London, Loughborough,
Manchester, Newcastle,
Northumbria, Nottingham,
Nottingham Trent, Oxford,
Oxford Brookes, Sheffield,
Southampton, Strathclyde,
Surrey, Swansea, Warwick
Please check with your university
careers service for details of events.

Application deadline
Year-round recruitment

Contact Details

✉ graduates@atkinsglobal.com

Turn to page 224 now to request
more information about Atkins.

Atkins provides professional design and engineering
consultancy services. They are a major player in a diversity of
sectors including building design, highways, rail, aviation, water,
oil and gas, power, nuclear, defence and the environment.

As a multidisciplinary consultant, Atkins plays a key role in a host of high-
profile projects. They are the lead design and engineering consultant for the
world's largest transport infrastructure project, the Dubai Metro. Atkins is also
supporting Airbus in the development of the world's largest airliner, the A380,
alongside managing 23% of the UK's highways. They have also designed one
of the UK's most energy efficient major buildings at Northumbria University.
Sustainable features include rain water harvesting and roof solar collectors to
produce hot water, helping to make it around 40% more efficient than most
comparable buildings.

With such a breadth and depth of capabilities, Atkins offers unparalleled
opportunities to build a rewarding career. With Atkins, graduates can work
with 16,800 of the brightest people in the industry in 175+ offices around the
world, using skills developed at university to deliver innovative solutions to
their clients. Atkins provides continuing professional development through
accredited training, set out by professional institutes, in addition to personal
development events.

A company that's as committed to diversity as it is to excellence, Atkins
welcomes graduates into architecture, engineering, planning and surveying
roles. They also recruit from a variety of disciplines for their management
consultant and project management vacancies.

Plan Design Enable

Everyone likes to be motivated

Architects, Engineers, Planners & Surveyors

There will be lots to get excited about when you join Atkins. We're a true people business that's proud of its rich mix of talents – one where you'll be free to innovate, your opinions will count and everyone is easy to get on with.

Then there are our projects. We work on some of the world's most celebrated projects, but we also channel our expertise into local communities. So not only will your skills be continually stretched, but you could be making a real difference to society, as you learn from some of the best people in their fields and get the support you need to gain recognised professional accreditation.

Also, there are the rewards. You'll get everything your contribution deserves, including a generous 'golden hello' and competitive salary.

If you're motivated to join a company that's as committed to diversity as it is to excellence, find out more at our website.

www.atkinsglobal.com/graduates

You'll like it at Atkins

ΛTKINS

BAE SYSTEMS

Vacancies for around
300 graduates in 2008

- Engineering
- Finance
- General Management
- Human Resources
- Law
- Logistics
- Manufacturing
- Marketing
- Purchasing
- Research & Development
- Sales

Starting salary for 2008
£22,500

**Universities BAE Systems
plans to visit in 2007-8**
Aston, Bath, Birmingham,
Bristol, Brunel, Cambridge,
Cardiff, City, Durham,
Edinburgh, Glasgow,
Heriot-Watt, Lancaster,
Leeds, Leicester,
Liverpool, Loughborough,
Manchester, Nottingham,
Nottingham Trent,
Sheffield, Southampton,
Strathclyde, Warwick
Please check with your university
careers service for details of events.

Application deadline
Year-round recruitment
Application before December 2007
strongly recommended.

Contact Details
☎ 01772 677277

Turn to page 224 now to request more
information about BAE Systems.

In the exciting arena of international defence, BAE Systems is a leading player with a wealth of opportunities for graduates. They develop, deliver and support the world's most advanced defence and aerospace systems, in the air, on land and at sea.

BAE Systems recognise that no two people are alike, and aim to offer a range of career paths that appeal to a broad range of individuals.

BAE Systems have three graduate entry programmes; the Graduate Development Framework 'GDF', the Finance Leader Development Programme 'FLDP' and 'Sigma'.

The GDF could be a springboard to an amazing career with BAE Systems. Whether the path graduates choose is in one or more of the engineering disciplines (including Systems, Software, Mechanical, Electrical & Electronic, Structures and many more), or business roles such as Project Management, Commercial, Procurement, Human Resources or Sales and Marketing, the GDF offers the opportunity to develop personal competencies and business awareness that will complement graduates' initial professional development, working alongside other professionals in a truly multi-disciplinary environment.

The Finance Leader Development Programme (FLDP) is for those looking for a career in finance leadership and 'Sigma' for fast track international leadership.

BAE Systems offer an excellent package to new graduates, which includes a competitive salary (£22,500 to £26,500), an initial welcome payment of £2,000, final salary pension, 25 days' holiday and the opportunity to participate in healthcare and share schemes.

BAKER & McKENZIE

www.ukgraduates.bakernet.com

**Vacancies for around
38 graduates in 2008**
For training contracts starting in 2010

Law

Starting salary in 2008
£36,500

**Universities that
Baker & McKenzie
plans to visit in 2007-8**
Birmingham, Bristol,
Cambridge, Durham,
Exeter, Leeds, London,
Manchester, Nottingham,
Oxford, Warwick
Please check with your university
careers service for details of events.

Application deadline
See website for full details.

Contact Details
✉ london.graduate.recruit
@bakernet.com
Turn to page 224 now to request more
information about Baker & McKenzie.

Baker & McKenzie offers unparalleled opportunities to become
a first class lawyer in the world's largest global law firm. With a
network covering 70 locations in 38 countries and a presence
in virtually every important financial and commercial centre
worldwide, the firm is able to attract the highest quality
multi-jurisdictional clients.

Baker & McKenzie look for graduates who are stimulated by intellectual
challenge and want to be 'the best' at what they do. Effective communication,
the ability to be creative but practical problem solvers, and a sense of humour
are qualities which help applicants stand out from the crowd. In return,
trainees receive exceptional training – a commitment which recently lead to
the firm winning 'Best Trainer – Large City Firm' at the LCN-TSG Training and
Recruitment Awards for the fourth consecutive year.

Baker & McKenzie's future trainees receive tailored training during their LPC
year, at the College of Law's new centre in Moorgate. The course allows
the firm to build stronger links with its future trainees, whilst providing more
focused training, support and social contact.

The two year training programme commences with an interactive and practical
induction focusing on key skills – problem solving, interviewing, presenting
and IT. Trainees complete four six-month 'seats', gaining early responsibility
on high profile transactions. In addition to a core Corporate seat, trainees are
offered the opportunity to go on client or international secondments to such
locations as Sydney, Chicago, Moscow, Hong Kong and Tokyo.

Baker & McKenzie's commitment to training begins even before starting with
the firm through both London-based and International Summer Placements.

London

BAKER & McKENZIE

Expand your horizons

Baker & McKenzie in London offers unparalleled opportunities to become a first class lawyer in the world's largest global law firm.

Tel: +44 (0)20 7919 1000
Email: london.graduate.recruit@bakernet.com

WINNER LC-N
AWARDS
2007

BEST TRAINER
LARGE CITY FIRM

www.ukgraduates.bakernet.com

Bank of America

**Vacancies for around
100 graduates in 2008**

- Investment Banking
- IT

Bank of Opportunity™

Starting salary for 2008
£Competitive

**Universities that
Bank of America
plans to visit in 2007-8**
Bristol, Cambridge, Dublin,
London, Manchester,
Oxford, Warwick
Please check with your university
careers service for details of events.

Application deadline
14th November 2007

Contact Details
✉ emea.university@
bankofamerica.com
Turn to page 224 now to request more
information about Bank of America.

Bank of America is the largest bank in the world by tier 1
capital and the fifth most profitable company in the world.
Bank of America is also the second largest bank in the U.S.
in terms of revenues.

The company's Global Corporate and Investment Banking group (GCIB)
focuses on companies with annual revenues of more than US$2.5 million;
middle-market and large corporations; institutional investors; financial
institutions; and government entities. GCIB provides innovative services in
M&A, equity and debt capital raising, lending, trading, risk management,
treasury management and research. Bank of America serves clients in 175
countries and has relationships with 79 percent of the Global Fortune 500.

The Bank's international growth strategy is to build a profitable universal bank
with Global Markets as a core competency. Bank of America targets European
clients with strong U.S. interests and issuer and investor clients with whom the
bank already has a strong relationship in the U.S.

The bank's long-term senior debt is rated Aa2 by Moody's, AA- by Standard &
Poor's and AA- by Fitch.

The Bank's culture offers new joiners the opportunity to enjoy meaningful
interaction with both clients and senior executives in a personal and
collaborative atmosphere.

Initial training takes place in New York or Charlotte and combines classroom
training with group and individual projects led by industry experts. Graduates
will learn technical, personal and professional skills and also more about Bank
of America's capabilities and culture.

Opportunity Starts Here®

Imagine what you could achieve as an analyst at Bank of America, an entrepreneurial organisation that is among the top five most profitable companies in the world. From London to New York to cities across 175 countries, we are leading some of the largest, most complex deals in global corporate and investment banking today. To learn about our competitive edge and what it means for your career, visit bankofamerica.com/careers.

Bank of America
Bank of Opportunity™

bankofamerica.com/careers

BARCLAYS
Now there's a thought

Vacancies for around 140 graduates in 2008

- Accountancy
- Finance
- General Management
- Human Resources
- IT
- Marketing
- Retailing
- Sales

Starting salary for 2008
£24,000
Plus £3,500 joining bonus and £3,550 mobility allowance.

Universities Barclays Bank plans to visit in 2007-8
Aberdeen, Aston, Bath, Belfast, Bristol, Cambridge, Durham, Edinburgh, Glasgow, Leeds, London, Loughborough, Manchester, Newcastle, Nottingham, Oxford, Reading, Strathclyde, Warwick, York
Please check with your university careers service for details of events.

Application deadline
31st December 2007

Contact Details
✉ barclays.graduates@reed.co.uk

Turn to page 224 now to request more information about Barclays Bank.

Throughout their history, Barclays' sprit of innovation has inspired groundbreaking ideas that have moved the entire industry forward. They were the first bank to issue a credit card, launch cashpoint machines, set up a website and offer a carbon-neutral debit card. Not surprisingly, their fresh-thinking approach also makes them an inspirational place to develop a graduate career.

That could be in Business Banking, Retail Banking, Barclaycard, Tax, Treasury, Finance, IT, HR, Marketing and Chief Administration Office. Each business area runs its own structured training programme lasting between one and three years. Graduates will get a real insight into how the area operates, enjoy a high profile and learn from business leaders.

Barclays look for a strong academic background. But the right attitude is just as important as a quick brain. Graduates must be ambitious and focused with the drive and initiative to improve on what's gone before. What has been done outside of academia – placements, gap years, voluntary work or sporting or cultural activities for example – will also help Barclays decide whether applicants have the potential to make a real impact on their business.

Expect formal training, on-the-job learning, study leave to help gain professional qualifications and up to £2,000 to invest in personal development that's relevant to the role. What's more, graduate development won't stop when the programme ends. Career-long learning is a way of life at Barclays and will encourage successful applicants to really make a mark and get on.

Moment of inspiration
9th September 1986. New York.

Our Chairman buys 100 Barclays shares, making us the first British bank to be traded on the New York Stock Exchange

A few weeks earlier we were also the first British bank to be listed on the Tokyo stock exchange. Two initiatives that underlined our growing global status and our ambitions to expand internationally. Today we operate across 50 countries and look after the finances of 27 million customers. But you won't join us because we're big (although that has its advantages). You'll be more attracted to us because we're bold. And you like the idea of helping us get there first: whether 'there' is a new place, a new product or a whole new way of doing things. Find out more at www.inspiredbybarclays.com

---

Graduate Careers in Business Banking, Retail Banking, Barclaycard, Tax, Treasury, Finance, IT, HR, Marketing and Chief Administration Office

---

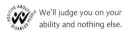

BARCLAYS
Now there's a thought

BARCLAYS CAPITAL

Vacancies for around 600 graduates in 2008

■ Accountancy
■ Consulting
■ Finance
■ General Management
■ Investment Banking

Vacancies also available in Europe, Asia and the USA.

Starting salary for 2008
£Competitive

Universities that Barclays Capital plans to visit in 2007-8

Cambridge, Dublin, Durham, Glasgow, London, Manchester, Nottingham, Oxford, Strathclyde, Warwick
Please check with your university careers service for details of events.

Application deadline
30th November 2007

Contact Details
Turn to page 224 now to request more information about Barclays Capital.

Be individual. Take charge. Expect challenge.

Barclays Capital is the investment banking division of Barclays Bank PLC which has an AA long-term credit rating and a balance sheet of over £996 billion (€1.4 trillion). With a distinctive business model, Barclays Capital provides large corporate, government and institutional clients with solutions to their financing and risk management needs.

Barclays Capital has offices in 26 countries, employs over 13,200 people and has the global reach and distribution power to meet the needs of issuers and investors worldwide. Their graduate programme is key to its success.

On the programme graduates are provided with an excellent understanding of financial markets, as well as the firm's products, instruments and services. This creates a strong platform on which to build more specialist expertise. The programme takes learning one step further, incorporating practical applications through a variety of case studies, workshops and presentations.

Depending on the area joined, each graduate receives comprehensive, role-specific training as well as training in soft skills. Barclays Capital also encourages people to obtain appropriate professional qualifications.

Barclays Capital is recruiting into the following areas: compliance, corporate communications, corporate real estate services, finance, global financial risk management, global marketing, human resources, information risk management, investment banking and debt capital markets, legal, operations, operational risk management, quantitative analytics, research, sales, strategy and planning, structuring, technology and trading.

And that's just the beginning.

Have a life.
Do things differently.
Feel supported.

Think about Barclays Capital.

Graduate and Intern Opportunities

BARCLAYS
CAPITAL

www.barclayscapital.com/campusrecruitment

BDO Stoy Hayward

**Vacancies for around
300 graduates in 2008**

- Accountancy
- Consulting
- Finance
- IT

WHAT IF PEOPLE ASKED HOW YOU WERE AND REALLY WANTED TO KNOW?

Starting salary for 2008
£Competitive

**Universities that
BDO Stoy Hayward
plans to visit in 2007-8**

Bath, Birmingham, Bristol,
Cambridge, Cardiff, Durham,
Edinburgh, Exeter, Leeds,
London, Loughborough,
Manchester, Nottingham,
Oxford, Reading, Sheffield,
Southampton, Surrey,
Warwick, York
Please check with your university
careers service for details of events.

Application deadline
Year-round recruitment

Contact Details
✉ student.recruitment@bdo.co.uk
☎ 020 7893 2085

Turn to page 224 now to request more
information about BDO Stoy Hayward.

BDO Stoy Hayward is the UK member firm of BDO International, the world's fifth largest accountancy network with more than 600 offices in 100 countries. They won the 'Accountancy Age Employer of the Year' award in 2006.

BDO Stoy Hayward have their own special culture. One that people enjoy working in, no matter what their background, age, sex or ethnicity. They want individuals who are bright and creative – who place importance on living their values and who appreciate and respect people – whoever they are and wherever they come from.

At BDO Stoy Hayward, every day is a preparation for the next. Training is made as flexible and appropriate as possible for all trainees. And BDO Stoy Hayward believes there is no substitute for first-hand experience.

The company's results are excellent. Most of their graduates study for the ACA, awarded by the Institute of Chartered Accountants for England and Wales. BDO Stoy Hayward also offer other routes to professional qualifications, depending on the business stream joined.

There are various opportunities available to employees to continue their development and career within the firm. These include opportunities to work on client projects with partners and colleagues in other business areas and international secondments. Additionally, BDO Stoy Hayward's broad client base means there are opportunities in many different businesses and sectors.

Graduate opportunities exist in a number of exciting areas from tax to forensic services. Visit www.bdo.co.uk/careers for more information on the opportunities available and to view profiles of some of their graduates.

WHAT IF THE SECRET OF SUCCESS WASN'T A SECRET?

BDO Stoy Hayward is the UK's fastest growing major accountancy firm and part of one of the world's leading international networks, with more than 600 offices in over 100 countries. Learning and training is the key to success in accountancy. We're keen that all our trainees reach qualification within three years. It'll be hard work, but our support means we have unusually high levels of qualification. Success is simple, with the right help. **Apply online at www.bdo.co.uk/careers**

YOU'LL NOTICE THE DIFFERENCE

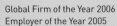

BDO Stoy Hayward
Chartered Accountants

Bloomberg

careers.bloomberg.com

Vacancies for around 400+ graduates in 2008

- ▊ Finance
- ▊ IT
- ▊ Media
- ▊ Research & Development
- ▊ Sales

Vacancies also available in Asia and the USA.

Starting salary for 2008
£Competitive

Universities Bloomberg plans to visit in 2007-8
Please check with your university careers service for details of events.

Application deadline
Year-round recruitment

Contact Details
Turn to page 224 now to request more information about Bloomberg.

Bloomberg is the leading global provider of data, news and analytics. The Bloomberg Professional® service and Bloomberg's media services provide real-time and archived financial and market data, pricing, trading, news and communications tools in a single, integrated package.

Bloomberg's clients include corporations, news organisations, financial and legal professionals, and individuals around the world. With over 9,000 employees operating in more than 127 countries, Bloomberg is truly international. The largest offices include New York, London and Tokyo, and this is where the majority of graduate opportunities are located.

Graduate positions include financial sales, software development, global data, IT, project management, news and many more. For most roles, a second language is desirable but not essential. Bloomberg recruits all year round and from any discipline. A passion for finance, technology or an international career is required. Bloomberg breaks down barriers between people and encourages communication by bringing colleagues together. With no job titles or executive areas, the culture fosters interaction at every level.

Bloomberg supports community programmes by reinvesting resources back into the society through sponsorships and employee volunteer activities. But the real depth and diversity of Bloomberg's way of life comes from the creativity and commitment of its people. Training is extensive and ongoing via Bloomberg University. Courses are wide-ranging and available to all, allowing graduates to progress quickly and take on real responsibility quickly. Opportunities are listed on the website and start dates are available throughout the year.

MOVE THE MARKETS.
Innovate from the front.

Join the company at the forefront of finance and technology.

Bloomberg provides information to business leaders around the world. Our employees have a passion for excellence, no matter what their experience is. We foster that passion and encourage growth and development in every way possible.

We have opportunities in Financial Sales, Data Analysis, Software Development, News and many more areas. Bloomberg is the ideal place for you to develop your knowledge and enthusiasm for the financial markets.

careers.bloomberg.com

bp

beyond petroleum

www.bp.com/careers

Vacancies for around
200+ graduates in 2008

- Accountancy
- Engineering
- Finance
- General Management
- Human Resources
- IT
- Purchasing

Starting salary for 2008
£28,000+

Universities that BP
plans to visit in 2007-8
Please check with your university
careers service for details of events.

Application deadline
See website for full details.

Contact Details
Turn to page 224 now to request
more information about BP.

How is enough energy provided to meet the demands of a
growing population without compromising the environment?
And at a time when many oil and gas-fields are reaching the end
of their lives? That's the challenge facing the energy industry
and BP today – and now there's the chance for graduates to
meet this challenge within a global blue-chip company.

Technical graduates can work with cutting-edge technology in geoscience and
engineering, including chemical, instrument, control and electrical, mechanical,
petroleum and drilling. For graduates who are excited by technology and look
for improvements at every turn, BP might be the right choice.

Graduates interested in business can move into high-profile areas such as:
marketing, operations, trading, finance, business analysis, digital business,
project evaluation, mergers and acquisitions, procurement and HR.

Whatever the position, all graduates are supported and encouraged to exceed
personal and professional targets by mentors and colleagues.

So what qualities are needed to succeed here? Certainly a passion and
drive to achieve the very best. That takes high-quality thinking and thought
leadership, as well as the ability to work well with colleagues, share information
and exchange ideas. While graduates come with a good level of technical
knowledge gained during their degree and from any work experience, BP
helps to nurture and build that expertise.

By joining BP, graduates gain the kind of training, support and progression
expected from a world-leading organisation, coupled with a range of
associated benefits. Because at the core of its success are its people.

When

we can't tell you what you'll
be doing tomorrow because
you've not come up with it yet.

Look beyond the limits.

We believe that what we are doing today will help us become the BP
we want to be tomorrow. Our business is the exploration, production,
refining, trading and distribution of energy; and we have nearly
100,000 people in 100 countries across six continents. In this age
of growing consumer demand and environmental urgency, we are
always looking to find new and better ways of delivering energy to
the world – without compromising the planet.

BP Ultimate offers more performance and less pollution than
ordinary fuels. New drilling processes mean we can access
otherwise inaccessible reserves of oil. We have a technology that
provides real-time data from a drill-head that is miles below ground
and hundreds of miles out to sea. Our Rhum field is a gas reservoir
240 miles off the Scottish coast that has become a world first. At the
same time we are doing everything possible to ensure every part
of our business operates to the highest safety standards.

This gives you a flavour of what we are doing today. But what
happens tomorrow is in your hands. We are looking for graduates to
take on roles within science, engineering and business in our four
operating divisions: Exploration & Production, Refining & Marketing,
Gas, Power & Renewables and Corporate. We want people who
don't see limits, only possibilities. **www.bp.com/careers**

bp

beyond petroleum

www.bt.com/grads

**Vacancies for around
250 graduates in 2008**

- Accountancy
- Consulting
- Engineering
- Finance
- General Management
- Human Resources
- IT
- Marketing
- Media
- Purchasing
- Research & Development
- Sales

Starting salary for 2008
£25,000

**Universities that BT
plans to visit in 2007-8**
Aston, Bath, Belfast,
Birmingham, Cambridge,
Cardiff, Dublin, Durham,
Edinburgh, Lancaster,
Leeds, Loughborough,
Manchester, Newcastle,
Nottingham, Oxford,
Sheffield, Southampton,
Ulster, Warwick
Please check with your university
careers service for details of events.

Application deadline
See website for full details.

Contact Details
Turn to page 224 now to request
more information about BT.

FIND OUT MORE
www.bt.com/grads

BT works with the world's most admired companies, providing ground-breaking communications and IT solutions in nearly 200 countries and across 5 continents. BT is widely admired for putting corporate social responsibility at the centre of everything the company does.

BT offers four different career paths for the graduate development programme: the professional services programme includes work in project management, business improvement and management consultancy; the ICT & Research programme is aiming to create software developers, researchers and network engineers; the functional specialists development programme includes roles in HR, marketing, finance or procurement (each leading to professional qualifications); the customer interface programme is ideal for those who understand the importance of putting customers at the heart of any business.

BT's two-year scheme is unusual for the fast-pace of entrants' development and the degree of responsibility from day one. Graduates will need at least a 2.1 honours degree or international equivalent in any degree discipline.

Benefits will include a starting salary from £25,000 with annual performance based bonuses, 27.5 days annual leave, sharesave and profit sharing schemes, an interest free loan and the BT Retirement Plan.

With rigorous support and coaching, the professional development programme will be carefully tailored to suit the successful applicant's strengths and chosen field.

BT is an equal opportunities employer.

Discover the real BT

Everyone knows BT, but you might not know all the things we're up to these days. From pioneering wi-fi communications and helping to count the Big Brother eviction votes to creating Vision, our new home entertainment service. We are changing the way people communicate in nearly 200 countries around the world.

Our graduates tell us that these are just some of the reasons they joined BT:

• The strength of our graduate programme
• The tailored support and training
• The real responsibility they receive from day one
• The chance to work on cutting-edge technology
• Our commitment to sustainability and CSR

Find out more about what you could be involved in as a graduate at bt.com/grads

How do medical staff talk on the move? We merged wi-fi and phone technology to create the Vocera. This hands-free device is as small as a badge and helps medical teams stay in touch, wherever they are.

Bringing it all together

INVESTOR IN PEOPLE

BT is an equal opportunity employer

Cadbury Schweppes

Vacancies for around 21 graduates in 2008

- Engineering
- Finance
- Human Resources
- Logistics
- Manufacturing
- Marketing
- Purchasing
- Research & Development
- Sales

Starting salary for 2008
£25,500

Universities that Cadbury Schweppes plans to visit in 2007-8

Aston, Bath, Birmingham, Bristol, Cambridge, Durham, Edinburgh, Leeds, London, Loughborough, Manchester, Nottingham, Oxford, Reading, Sheffield, Strathclyde, Surrey, Warwick
Please check with your university careers service for details of events.

Application deadline
See website for full details.

Contact Details

✉ csgraduates@csplc.com

☎ 0121 451 4164

Turn to page 224 now to request more information about Cadbury Schweppes.

Creating brands that are household names around the globe is no small feat. It takes highly commercial thinking, regular strokes of inventive genius and some truly great minds. As a blue-chip FTSE 100 company, Cadbury Schweppes has all of this. A market leader in every sense, they offer graduates the chance to build the career they've always wanted.

Cadbury Schweppes people have the satisfaction of working on some of the best-loved brands – everything from Bassett's Allsorts to Trident Soft and Cadbury Flake to Cadbury Creme Eggs. And, because this business was founded upon socially responsible principles that have been benefiting employees, suppliers and local communities for over 200 years, they're proud of what those brands stand for.

Graduates who share that passion have the chance to become part of the company's rich heritage, helping to develop an already famous portfolio as well as creating some new bestsellers. After all, many of their business leaders began their careers here. So people who are keen to learn and take on responsibility can go very far indeed. What makes the graduate scheme different is that it's uniquely tailored around the individual. That means a real, specially selected job from day one. And when the support of a mentor and enthusiastic colleagues is factored in, along with a competitive salary and great benefits, it makes a career at Cadbury Schweppes simply irresistible.

To find out more information on graduate careers and industrial placement opportunities visit www.cadburyschweppes.com/ukgraduates

irresistible

Each one of our famous brands is truly tempting. Just like our graduate scheme. Here you'll become a part of the prestigious business behind the likes of Cadbury Dairy Milk, Trident and Bassett's. As a global leader with a creative edge that keeps us at the forefront of the industry, not to mention our rich heritage and ethical standards to be proud of, we have a lot to offer. You'll find challenging and responsible roles and a tailored development programme for the career you've always wanted.

The chosen few who join us will need that extra half glass of talent. After all, we have a habit of spotting the next market leader.

YOU'LL REALLY WANT THIS
www.cadburyschweppes.com/ukgraduates

CANCER RESEARCH UK

Vacancies for around 100+ graduates in 2008

- Accountancy
- Finance
- General Management
- Human Resources
- IT
- Law
- Media
- Purchasing
- Retailing

Starting salary for 2008
£Competitive

Universities that Cancer Research UK plans to visit in 2007-8
Cambridge, Edinburgh, London, Manchester, Oxford
Please check with your university careers service for details of events.

Application deadline
See website for full details.

Contact Details
Turn to page 224 now to request more information about Cancer Research UK.

Cancer Research UK is the world's leading independent organisation dedicated to cancer research. Over 3,000 of the world's best doctors, nurses and scientific staff work on their pioneering research. But equally important are the dedicated individuals in fundraising, marketing, HR, communications, IT, finance and other support functions.

Last year, their income topped £420 million – an achievement that underlines the business expertise, commercial vision and marketing talent that supports the groundbreaking research work at their world-class centre of scientific excellence. So wherever graduates join them they can expect to make a real contribution from day one. And to help successful applicants achieve their own ambitions, they will benefit from a unique combination of on-the-job learning and formal, professional training.

Clearly, a career with Cancer Research UK offers plenty in the way of personal fulfilment. But what many people overlook is how commercially challenging and professionally rewarding their work can be. So while empathy for the cause is important, above all they're looking for ambitious, business-minded graduates who can help drive the organisation forward in the months and years to come.

Every year, Cancer Research UK offers a variety of graduate opportunities in all aspects of their work, including fundraising, science and corporate support services. To find out more about specific opportunities, visit their website. Graduates can also sign up for email alerts which will keep them up to date with any relevant vacancies at http://jobs.cancerresearchuk.org/alerts_signup_form.php

How many graduates feel their job lets them grow?

It's a fact, that more and more graduates are actively seeking a different job with better opportunities for progression. This just shows the importance of finding a career that will stretch you. Happily, that's exactly what we can offer you.

When you join one of our programmes, you'll start a high-level career at the forefront of your field. Not only will you benefit from a unique combination of on-the-job learning and comprehensive training, but you'll also be making a difference to thousands of cancer sufferers and their families. How many graduates can say that?

Start by visiting **http://jobs.cancerresearchuk.org**

Together we will beat cancer

Capgemini

CONSULTING.TECHNOLOGY.OUTSOURCING

www.uk.capgemini.com/careers/graduate

Vacancies for around 80 graduates in 2008

◼ Consulting
◼ IT

Starting salary for 2008
£25,000-£32,000

Universities Capgemini plans to visit in 2007-8
Aston, Bath,
Birmingham, Brunel,
Cambridge, Edinburgh,
London, Loughborough,
Manchester, Nottingham,
Oxford, Warwick
Please check with your university careers service for details of events.

Application deadline
Year-round recruitment

Contact Details
✉ graduate.careers.uk@ capgemini.com
☎ 020 7434 2171
Turn to page 224 now to request more information about Capgemini.

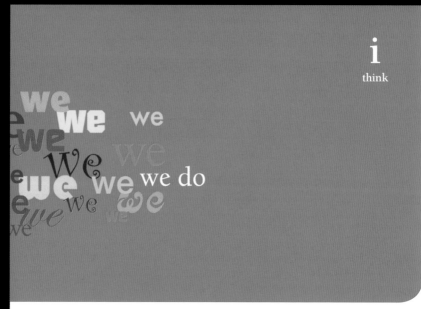

i
think

Capgemini has always believed in the power of collaboration. For over 40 years they've embraced this philosophy, helping companies worldwide address their business and IT issues through consulting, technology and outsourcing services.

In fact, at the heart of Capgemini's success is something they call the Collaborative Business Experience, a unique way of working that's designed to help clients achieve better, faster, more sustainable results. With 75,000 employees now helping businesses across over 30 countries, it's a strategy that's clearly working.

It's this sense of collaboration and community that makes Capgemini's Graduate Management Consultancy Programme such an attractive proposition too. From day one graduates will really feel like one of the team. They will be involved in key projects across Transformation and Business Consulting in a range of industries (everything from finance through to manufacturing and retail). Capgemini will listen to their ideas and share its collective experience too, helping graduates become first class management consultants.

Equally inclusive, Capgemini's technology services practice employs experts dedicated to everything from devising initial strategies right through to overseeing systems operations for its clients. So its Graduate Technology Consulting Programme will provide graduates with the opportunity to gain experience across a wide range of technologies, projects and business sectors. Graduates will be working in partnership with some of the world's largest and most prestigious organisations too, designing, building and running IT solutions. And, along the way, they will develop skills in programming, project management, systems development, testing and technical support.

i
still haven't found
what i'm looking for

we have

It's called the power of collaboration. The basic principle that, collectively, we're smarter than any one of us. It has helped us become one of the world's largest business & technology consulting firms. And it makes for a consulting career with more colour, camaraderie and creativity. There's amazing variety too. Graduates on the **Management Consulting** programme can be involved in strategy and transformation projects in every facet of businesses in every sector. Those who join the **Technology Consulting** programme will gain experience across an unparalleled range of technologies and roles, from programming and development to project management or infrastructure design. Either way, you'll be in the company of 75,000 very bright people having the time of their lives while changing how the world works. Isn't that exactly what you're looking for?

Have a look at our website,
and you'll see a future that's **brighter altogether**.

www.brighteraltogether.co.uk

Capgemini
CONSULTING.TECHNOLOGY.OUTSOURCING

Vacancies for around
250 graduates in 2008

- Human Resources
- Investment Banking
- IT

Vacancies also available in Europe, Asia, the USA and elsewhere in the world.

Starting salary for 2008
£Competitive

Universities that Citi plans to visit in 2007-8

Bath, Belfast, Bristol, Cambridge, Dublin, Edinburgh, Glasgow, London, Manchester, Oxford, St Andrews, Ulster, Warwick
Please check with your university careers service for details of events.

Application deadline
4th November 2007

Contact Details

Turn to page 224 now to request more information about Citi.

Are you ready to make your mark?

Citi is the most complete financial partner to individuals, corporations, financial institutions, institutional investors and governments in the world. Citi's Markets and Banking division is a global leader in banking, capital markets, and transaction services, with a presence in many countries dating back more than 100 years.

Citi enables clients to achieve their strategic financial objectives by providing them with cutting-edge ideas, best-in-class products and solutions, and unparalleled access to capital and liquidity.

This is a world-class firm that actively seeks to recruit the best. Working at Citi means embracing stimulating and challenging work, being at the centre of the financial industry, and having the chance to have a truly global career. It demands candidates who will thrive in this environment, who have an excellent academic background, the ability to work independently as well as in teams, and perform under pressure. Having a genuine passion for the industry is critical to becoming a successful Analyst.

Citi has been unwavering in their commitment to investing in their Analyst programmes. Ensuring all Analysts have superior financial knowledge and are equipped with the necessary skills is vital to successfully developing and maintaining profitable client relationships.

Citi believes in providing outstanding people with the best opportunity to realise their potential. They recruit into a broad range of business areas and from all degree disciplines, please visit www.careers.citigroup.com to find out more information about the opportunities that are available.

Just going with a name.

Going where you'll make a name for yourself.

Your Name Here

Markets & Banking

Citigroup Inc.

What do you want to accomplish? An impressive title, or something more? Last year one of our colleagues helped broker a deal that helped an African country reduce its debt portfolio through payment restructuring – only six months after graduation. Call us when you're ready to make your mark.

- Investment Banking
- Corporate Banking
- Capital Markets
- Sales & Trading
- Global Transaction Services
- Technology
- Human Resources
- Operations

apply online at careers.citigroup.com

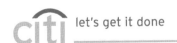

citi let's get it done

CIVIL SERVICE FASTSTREAM

www.faststream.gov.uk

Vacancies for around 500 graduates in 2008

- General Management
- IT

Vacancies also available in Europe.

Starting salary for 2008
£25,000-£27,000

Universities that the Fast Stream plans to visit in 2007-8
Aberystwyth, Bath, Birmingham, East Anglia, Lancaster, Liverpool, London, Newcastle, Nottingham, Oxford, Oxford Brookes, Sheffield, Warwick, York
Please check with your university careers service for details of events.

Application deadline
30th November 2007
See website for full details.

Contact Details
✉ faststream@parity.net
☎ 01276 400333
Turn to page 224 now to request more information about Fast Stream.

Who actually deals with the issues raised in the headlines? Who decides how to combat climate change; or on security provision for the 2012 Olympic Games? Who delivers a step-change in services to the public? Who represents the UK on the world scene? The Civil Service.

The Civil Service Fast Stream is a training and development programme for graduates with the potential to reach the top. Fast Streamers are groomed for senior management positions. From the outset, graduates move regularly between projects to acquire a range of business skills. They'll also be given considerable responsibility early on. Later, graduates will focus on one of three career groups: corporate services, operational delivery or policy delivery – but to reach the top they'll need experience in more than one area.

The Fast Stream is no easy option. Graduates need to be thorough, articulate and persuasive with a minimum 2:2 in any discipline and an intelligent, analytical and open-minded approach. Above all, they'll need to be the kind of person who gets results, able to deliver high-quality services to the public.

The training programme is exemplary and tailored to meet individual needs, combining on-the-job training and formal courses. Regardless of gender, ethnic origin, disability, age, sexuality or marital status, the Fast Stream looks forward to applications from people who have what it takes to make a difference.

The Fast Stream offers many opportunities, including schemes for economists, statisticians and technology in business. For other Civil Service opportunities, visit www.careers.civil-service.gov.uk

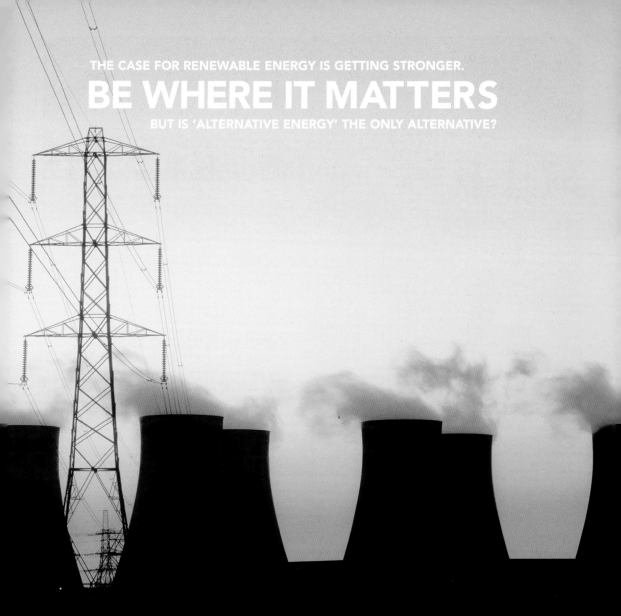

THE CASE FOR RENEWABLE ENERGY IS GETTING STRONGER.

BE WHERE IT MATTERS

BUT IS 'ALTERNATIVE ENERGY' THE ONLY ALTERNATIVE?

At the heart of government, tackling the biggest issues, our greatest resource is ideas. So as a Civil Service Fast Streamer, you'll find there's a genuine desire here to harness what's on your mind. You will be able to ask questions and be exposed to new challenges; this will give you the skills to develop and the opportunities to advance. Gender, age, race, sexual orientation and disability are irrelevant – it's your ability and outlook that interest us. Please apply online at www.faststream.gov.uk between 17th September and 30th November. Alternatively, please call 01276 400333 to receive a brochure.

CLIFFORD CHANCE

www.cliffordchance.com/gradsuk

Vacancies for around
130 graduates in 2008
For training contracts starting in
August 2010/February 2011

■ Law

Starting salary for 2008
£35,700

Universities that
Clifford Chance
plans to visit in 2007-8
Please check with your university
careers service for details of events.

Application deadline
Year-round recruitment
See website for full details.

Contact Details
✉ contacthr@cliffordchance.com
☎ 020 7006 6006
Turn to page 224 now to request more
information about Clifford Chance.

Clifford Chance is a truly global law firm, which operates as one organisation throughout the world. Their aim is to provide the highest quality professional advice by combining technical expertise with an appreciation of the commercial environment in which their clients work.

As a trainee lawyer, graduates will gain breadth and depth in their experiences. Clifford Chance offers a uniquely global perspective and actively encourages their lawyers to develop international experience. Most trainees interested in an international secondment spend six months abroad.

With offices in 20 countries, the firm operates across all business cultures and offers full service advice to clients in key financial and regulatory centres in Europe, the Americas and Asia. Clifford Chance's lawyers advise internationally and domestically, under both common and civil law systems. Their working style is characterised by a real sense of energy, enthusiasm, and determination to provide the best possible service to their clients.

Clifford Chance's recruitment strategy is based on a long-term view. They want graduates to stay with them on qualification, and enjoy a rewarding career contributing to the success of the global business. They are a diverse multicultural firm and expect and encourage their trainees to develop in directions that reflect their individual talents and style.

Throughout their training contract, the firm will give trainees the opportunity to realise their highest ambitions and become part of their commitment to be the world's premier law firm.

You know what you have in mind.
Now see where you'll find it.

What do you want from your future? A career exploring the kind of opportunities that only one of the world's most successful and respected law firms can offer? To receive outstanding training and rewards? To do interesting and important work that helps shape the face of global commerce?

To work with exceptional, down-to-earth people who share a passion for law and are committed to your success? To play an important part in the community and achieve your highest ambitions?

Given the choice, wouldn't you want it all?

To find out more about a career in law at Clifford Chance, visit
www.cliffordchance.com/gradsuk

THE TIMES
GRADUATE RECRUITMENT
AWARDS 2006
EMPLOYER OF CHOICE

Graduate Employer of Choice
for Law – 2005 and 2006

Clifford Chance LLP.

CLIFFORD
CHANCE

We have a global commitment to diversity, dignity and inclusiveness.

The co-operative

The **co-operative** 4,000 of our outlets are powered by renewable energy.

With nine different businesses, 4,500 outlets and 87,000 people, The Co-operative Group isn't just a food retailer but also a travel provider, a funeral director, a pharmacist, a legal services provider, and much more. But the real difference lies not just in what they do; it's what they are – a co-operative (and the world's largest consumer co-operative at that).

Unlike a plc, they do not just exist to make profit. Everything they do is for the benefit of their members and the community as a whole. They are driven by social goals and their co-operative values give them a positive advantage – for instance, they already sell more Fairtrade products than any other retailer.

But that doesn't mean they are any less ambitious – they still offer the depth and breadth of challenge you'd expect from a commercially-focussed business.

For those who want to pursue a rewarding career without compromising their values, the Group offers two programmes: business management and finance.

Rather than simply rotating from function to function, if graduates choose the business programme, they'll lead business critical projects (covering everything from marketing to HR) that have been hand picked to meet their specific development needs. Alternatively, for those with a passion for finance, graduates might want to consider their CIMA accredited programme. This offers four nine-month placements, where specialist knowledge in functions ranging from internal audit to tax will be gained.

Either way, graduates will gain experience across a number of businesses and enjoy all the support they'll need to drive their own career.

The **co-operative**

We're **a £9 billion business**
We're **4.5 million members**
We're **87,000 colleagues**
We're **4,500 outlets**
We're **one unique graduate employer**

As the world's largest consumer co-operative we can offer you a graduate experience that is altogether different. Our 9 different businesses – that vary from food to pharmacy, and from funerals to travel – will all be vying for your talents. Choosing the business critical projects that you work on, you'll ensure that the entire experience meets your career ambitions. But the real difference is, you'll be part of a co-operative. This means you'll be joining a business that's as ethically minded as it is commercially focused – perfect if you want to achieve your goals without compromising your values.

Discover our graduates' **altogether**|different
experiences at www.altogetherdifferent.com

corus

**Vacancies for around
140 graduates in 2008**

- Engineering
- Finance
- Human Resources
- Logistics
- Manufacturing
- Marketing
- Purchasing
- Research & Development

Starting salary for 2008
£19,500-£21,500

**Universities that Corus
plans to visit in 2007-8**
Aston, Bath, Birmingham,
Cambridge, Cardiff, Durham,
Lancaster, Leeds, Leicester,
Liverpool, London,
Loughborough, Manchester,
Newcastle, Northumbria,
Nottingham, Oxford,
Sheffield, Strathclyde,
Swansea, Warwick
Please check with your university
careers service for details of events.

Application deadline
See website for full details.

Contact Details
✉ recruitment@corusgroup.com
☎ 01926 488025

Turn to page 224 now to request
more information about Corus.

Corus is an international metals company that will provide
the opportunity to learn, develop, gain experience, broaden
horizons and make an impact. They have the scope to provide
individually tailored careers that will be interesting, challenging
and dynamic with commitment to professional accreditation,
joint career ownership and real work projects from the outset.

In order to maintain the position as a world class company, people who can
set goals and surpass them are essential; with drive, enthusiasm, ideas,
commitment and flexibility. Successful graduates are those who benchmark
their own achievements against those of peers, respect the community around
them and simply work hard.

Corus is renowned for creating value. Company culture is one of continuous
improvement and open communication with a strong focus on safety and
sustainability. Efforts and commitment of Corus employees in 2006 resulted in
turnover of £10.3 billion.

Innovative projects Corus are involved in include the elimination of hexavalent
chromium in consumer goods which causes white rust in storage and steel
protective barriers at Westminster designed for security critical situations.
The Sky Plaza in Hong Kong, National Convention Centre in Vietnam, Rotana
Hotel in Dubai, Terminal 3 at Charles de Gaulle Airport in Paris, Taipei Arena in
Taiwan and Imperial War Museum in Manchester all have Corus expertise and
metal in common. Corus also has major contracts with Airbus, Land Rover
Discovery, Bugatti Veyron, Network Rail, Bosch, Ikea and John West to name
just a few.

corus

Leading by example

We are currently involved in projects such as the Qizhong International Tennis Centre Shanghai, the Fusionpolis landmark in Singapore, Delhi metro in India and new Bank of America Building in New York.

To help us maintain our position as a world class company, we recruit into 10 different areas, varying from Engineering to Commercial and Supplies Management to RD&T to Finance – to name but a few. To take the company forward successfully, we need people who have drive, enthusiasm, ideas, commitment, flexibility, imagination and resilience.

In return we offer a renowned graduate programme tailored to your individual and function needs with opportunities to learn, develop, gain experience and make your mark.

All applications are online. To find out more about how Corus can meet your aspirations, and to register your interest in a graduate career or undergraduate placement, please visit our website.

Benefits include competitive salary, bonus scheme, 35 days holiday, employee share-save schemes and interest-free loan.

Corus Value in steel

For more information, contact:
T: 01926 488025
www.corusgroupcareers.com

CREDIT SUISSE

www.credit-suisse.com/careers

**Vacancies for around
200 graduates in 2008**

- Finance
- Investment Banking
- IT

Vacancies also available in Asia,
the USA and elsewhere in the world.

Starting salary for 2008
£Competitive

**Universities Credit Suisse
plans to visit in 2007-8**
Bath, Bristol, Cambridge,
London, Manchester,
Oxford, Warwick
Please check with your university
careers service for details of events.

Application deadline
23rd November 2007

Contact Details
Turn to page 224 now to request more
information about Credit Suisse.

Credit Suisse provides investment banking, private banking and asset management services to clients across the world. Active in over fifty countries and employing more than 45,000 people, Credit Suisse is one of the world's leading banks.

In 2006, Credit Suisse celebrated its 150th anniversary with an announcement of record profits and the launch of its integrated banking model delivering comprehensive financial solutions to a diverse global client base. There are exceptional opportunities for further growth in new product areas and emerging markets; there are equally exceptional opportunities for the people who can deliver that growth.

Credit Suisse offers intellectual challenges, high rewards and global development potential for individuals who share an enthusiasm for business-critical innovation. There are opportunities in investment banking (including fixed income and equities), Asset Management, Information Technology and other support functions, as well as a range of internships and industrial placements.

Credit Suisse training programs are designed to be best in class. Content varies among business areas, but all programs combine formal learning with on-the-job practice and personal coaching to create an environment for further development. The Bank's award-winning Business School encourages learning and growth throughout one's career.

Most people who join Credit Suisse do so because of 'the people'. The Bank appeals to intelligent and outgoing personalities who want to work together in an atmosphere of co-operation and respect. It's a different perspective on how a big bank should go about its business, but it works for Credit Suisse.

Some think
steel and glass.

We think
meeting
of minds.

Mention global finance and people will often think of big buildings of glass
and steel, marble halls and swift lifts. But offices are only offices and we
have to work somewhere. It's what we do inside those offices that matters.
Banking adds value, creates wealth and makes things happen in the world.
The people at Credit Suisse do important, exhilarating, rewarding work,
but they are still just people. So if you're thinking that the high-rise world
of global finance is not for you, give us the benefit of the doubt and visit
the website. You might feel right at home.

www.credit-suisse.com/careers

CREDIT SUISSE

Thinking New Perspectives.

Deloitte.

www.deloitte.co.uk/graduates

Vacancies for around 1,200 graduates in 2008

- Accountancy
- Consulting
- Finance
- IT

Starting salary for 2008
£Competitive

Universities that Deloitte plans to visit in 2007-8

Aberdeen, Aston, Bath, Belfast, Birmingham, Bristol, Cambridge, Cardiff, City, Dublin, Durham, East Anglia, Edinburgh, Exeter, Glasgow, Lancaster, Leeds, Leicester, Liverpool, London, Loughborough, Manchester, Newcastle, Nottingham, Oxford, Reading, Sheffield, Southampton, St Andrews, Strathclyde, Warwick, York
Please check with your university careers service for details of events.

Application deadline
Year-round recruitment

Contact Details

✉ gradrec.uk@deloitte.co.uk

☎ 0800 323 333

Turn to page 224 now to request more information about Deloitte.

Deloitte offers graduates a challenging, but highly rewarding career within the professional services industry. The depth and breadth of their expertise allows them to offer their clients an unrivalled service. They're a world-class firm with a network of UK offices and an abundance of career paths and opportunities.

Talent is the lifeblood of the firm. Deloitte employs people who are great and make them exceptional. The training and development programmes they provide are second-to-none and will guarantee that graduates become highly skilled and well-rounded business professionals. They nurture talent both formally and informally with programmes that are tailor-made for each individual. From the Summer Vacation Scheme to their workshadow days, there are many ways to find out what working with Deloitte is really like, even before graduation.

Deloitte has a huge number of bright individuals working for them in the UK. All that talent and flair makes Deloitte a particularly invigorating place to be. Their culture encourages that rare state of equilibrium where hard work really is balanced by enjoying a life outside of work. They believe in plain speaking, pragmatic thinking and delivering on their promises, both to one another and to their clients. All of which makes Deloitte a special place to work.

Deloitte recruits graduates with a minimum of 300 UCAS tariff points and a predicted or obtained 2:1 in any discipline. Deloitte welcomes applications for deferred entry.

Apply online at www.deloitte.co.uk/graduates. For Consulting only, the deadline is 31st January 2008.

If you once imagined yourself as a rock 'n' roll legend…

…don't worry. You can still make a name for yourself in the music business.

Aspirations drive individuals and businesses. By constantly fulfilling ours, we've kept ahead in the global marketplace for professional services. It's the aspiration and ambitions of exceptional individuals like you that have helped us achieve our goals.

For you, a childhood dream of playing to stadium crowds could become the reality of providing vital business advice to some of the biggest names in the music business.

Wherever your aspirations take you within Deloitte, you'll have the promise of a career that can take you further – and faster – than you ever thought possible.

www.deloitte.co.uk/graduates

A career worth aspiring to

Deloitte.

Audit . Tax . Consulting . Corporate Finance .

Deutsche Bank /

www.db.com/careers

Vacancies for around 600 graduates in 2008

- Accountancy
- Finance
- Human Resources
- Investment Banking
- IT
- Law

Starting salary for 2008
£Competitive

Universities Deutsche Bank plans to visit in 2007-8
Please check with your university careers service for details of events.

Application deadline
1st November 2007

Contact Details
Turn to page 224 now to request more information about Deutsche Bank.

Deutsche Bank is committed to being the best financial services provider in the world. And, as an aspirational employer with the platform to lift careers to the next level, it fosters a diverse, inclusive work environment that encourages new ideas. It prides itself on building a long-term relationship with its employees.

Deutsche Bank's drive to be the best financial services provider has gained it numerous accolades. In 2005, in recognition of its outstanding performance, it was awarded the title of "Bank of the Year" by International Financing Review (IFR) for the second time in three years – the only bank to have ever achieved this. In 2006, it won all the major deals of the year awards from IDD and in 2007, swept the board at the Lipper and ISR Awards.

At Deutsche Bank 'A Passion to Perform' is more than just a claim – it's the way it does business, attracting the brightest talent to deliver an unmatched franchise. Its breadth of experience, leading-edge capabilities and financial strength create value for all its stakeholders: clients, investors, employees, and society as a whole.

Even though the bank continues to evolve and change, the key to Deutsche Bank's success remains constant: a focus on client needs, a spirit of innovation, a broad range of expertise combined with technological power and financial strength delivered by diverse, highly-skilled professionals across the globe.

Deutsche Bank is continually visiting the leading campuses around the world searching for talent. It is looking for fresh ideas, innovative solutions and an entrepreneurial spirit.

Your vision: To reach for the top.
Our promise: Lifting you even higher.

You thrive on achievement and you want to see just how far your talent will take you. We do too.
That's why, at Deutsche Bank, you'll be given the opportunity to realize your greatest ambitions.
As one of the world's leading financial institutions, we have the platform to take your career higher.
You will be part of an innovative, modern corporate culture that celebrates achievement.

Join us in: Asset Management – Finance – Global Banking – Global Markets – Human Resources –
Operations – Private Wealth Management – Legal, Risk & Capital – Technology.

Expect the better career.

Find out more at **www.db.com/careers**

A Passion to Perform.　　Deutsche Bank

DLA PIPER

www.dlapiper.com

Vacancies for around 95 graduates in 2008
For training contracts starting in 2010

■ Law

Starting salary for 2008
£Competitive

Universities DLA Piper plans to visit in 2007-8
Aberdeen, Birmingham,
Bristol, Cambridge,
Cardiff, Dundee, Durham,
Edinburgh, Exeter, Glasgow,
Hull, Leeds, Leicester,
Liverpool, London,
Manchester, Newcastle,
Nottingham, Oxford,
Sheffield, St Andrews,
Strathclyde, Warwick, York
Please check with your university
careers service for details of events.

Application deadline
31st July 2008

Contact Details
✉ recruitment.graduate@
 dlapiper.com
☎ 020 7796 6677
Turn to page 224 now to request
more information about DLA Piper.

DLA Piper is one of the world's largest legal services organisations with more than 3,000 lawyers across 24 countries providing a broad range of advice through their global practice groups. Their current vision is to be the leading global business law firm.

In 2006 The Lawyer awarded DLA Piper 'Global Law Firm of the Year' at their annual awards, proving they are moving closer to that vision. Clients include some of the world's leading businesses, governments, banks and financial institutions. DLA Piper offers trainees in all UK offices the opportunity to apply for various international secondments.

A number of independent bodies, including The Financial Times, recognise DLA Piper as being a good place to work. They also hold the 'Investors in People' accreditation, demonstrating commitment to their employees and their ongoing development.

There is no 'standard' DLA Piper trainee, however they do require a strong academic background and look for good communicators and team players. As well as this, in line with the firm's main focus of work, a keen interest in the corporate world is essential – as is an appetite for life!

Trainees complete four six-month seats and progress is monitored through regular reviews and feedback. The in-house Professional Skills Course combined with high-quality on-the-job experience means an excellent grounding on which DLA Piper's trainees build their professional careers. In 2007 nearly 90% of DLA Piper's qualifying trainees stayed with the firm.

BE LOCAL – GO GLOBAL

≡ıı ERNST & YOUNG

Vacancies for around 750 graduates in 2008

- Accountancy
- Consulting
- Finance
- IT

Starting salary for 2008
£Competitive

Universities Ernst & Young plans to visit in 2007-8
Aberdeen, Aston, Bath, Birmingham, Bristol, Brunel, Cambridge, Cardiff, Durham, Edinburgh, Essex, Exeter, Glasgow, Heriot-Watt, Lancaster, Leeds, Leicester, Liverpool, London, Loughborough, Manchester, Newcastle, Nottingham, Oxford, Reading, Sheffield, Southampton, St Andrews, Strathclyde, Warwick, York
Please check with your university careers service for details of events.

Application deadline
Year-round recruitment

Contact Details
✉ gradrec@uk.ey.com
☎ 0800 289 208

Turn to page 224 now to request more information about Ernst & Young.

It's a funny thing, potential. Lots of things have it but, to turn it into reality, they all need advice, support and guidance from people that know the territory inside out.

Ernst & Young has 114,000 people, in 700 locations across 140 countries around the world that are working to help companies realise the potential in their business – with support in audit, assurance, tax, corporate finance and business advisory.

Graduates get access to a breadth and depth of experience that's unparalleled, to help realise their own unique potential. Early on, they work with real clients, with real problems, to help companies overcome the challenges they face and get the most from their business. With first rate training and coaching experiences behind them, when Ernst & Young graduates say something, people have the confidence that what they're saying is right.

Every single person at the firm has a dedicated counselor and mentor to help them develop – from professional qualifications to the broader business skills needed to advise the biggest and the best. Clients want to deal with real people, not corporate clones, individual personalities matter a lot. Delivery to the highest standards, on time, every time ensures the flexibility to keep life in balance.

As well as graduate positions, there are work experience, summer internship and Industrial Placement Programmes. But for a career starting now, Ernst & Young has what graduates need to turn what they could be, into what they are.

"These days, when I surprise myself, I'm not surprised..."

We believe that most good people have it in them to become great people. And we know that it's in our interest to make that happen. That's why we support our people every inch of the way, encourage them to test their limits and always look to develop the qualities that got them here in the first place.
www.ey.com/uk/careers

INVESTOR IN PEOPLE

THE SUNDAY TIMES
20 BEST BIG COMPANIES TO WORK FOR 2007

ΞU ERNST & YOUNG
Quality In Everything We Do

EVERSHEDS

www.eversheds.com/graduaterecruitment

Vacancies for around 80 graduates in 2008
For training contracts starting in 2010

 Law

Starting salary for 2008
£34,000

Universities Eversheds plans to visit in 2007-8
Aberdeen, Aston, Bath, Belfast, Birmingham, Bristol, Cambridge, Cardiff, Dublin, Durham, East Anglia, Edinburgh, Exeter, Glasgow, Hull, Kent, Lancaster, Leeds, Leicester, Liverpool, London, Loughborough, Manchester, Northumbria, Nottingham, Nottingham Trent, Oxford, Southampton, St Andrews, Strathclyde, Swansea, Warwick, York
Please check with your university careers service for details of events.

Application deadline
Year-round recruitment

Contact Details
Turn to page 224 now to request more information about Eversheds.

Eversheds LLP is one of the largest full service international law firms in the world with over 4,000 people and 32 offices in major cities across the UK, Europe and Asia. They work for some of the world's most prestigious organisations in both the public and private sector, offering them a compelling mixture of straightforward advice, clear direction, predictable costs and outstanding service.

It's a winning combination that has meant they are now expanding quicker than any of their closest competitors. Eversheds act for 111 listed companies, including 43 FTSE 250 companies, 30 of the 37 British-based Fortune 500 companies and now have one of the fastest growing corporate teams in the City.

In 2006, Eversheds laid out a strategic plan that will see them build on these achievements and grow over the next few years into a major player on the legal stage around the world. They are looking for highly ambitious and focused trainees to help them achieve their goals.

Eversheds people are valued for their drive and legal expertise but also for their business advice too. They develop the same qualities in their trainees. Eversheds offer a full, well-rounded training programme with the opportunity to focus technical skills in each of the various practice groups as trainees rotate through four six month seats, while also taking part in a full programme of personal and commercial development skills training too, including finance and business, communication, presenting, business writing, client care, professional standards and advocacy.

In law there are no short cuts

But there are fast tracks

Eversheds is a major international law firm in the middle of an exhilarating phase of growth that will see us become a leading light on the global legal stage.

So, join us as a trainee and you are guaranteed a stimulating experience: opportunities and challenges will come thick and fast and our exceptionally talented team will involve you in diverse, high profile legal work.

We will give you the best possible start. And with good reason: by challenging and supporting our trainees in equal measures, we ensure that they stay on the fast track. Find out more by visiting our website.

 EVERSHEDS

www.eversheds.com

ExxonMobil

Vacancies for around 50 graduates in 2008

- Accountancy
- Engineering
- Finance
- Human Resources
- IT
- Marketing
- Retailing
- Sales

Starting salary for 2008
£30,000

Universities ExxonMobil plans to visit in 2007-8
Aberdeen, Bath, Belfast, Birmingham, Cambridge, Dublin, Heriot-Watt, London, Loughborough, Manchester, Newcastle, Nottingham, Oxford, Southampton, Strathclyde, Surrey
Please check with your university careers service for details of events.

Application deadline
See website for full details.

Contact Details
✉ exxonmobil@ workresourcing.com
☎ 0845 330 8878
Turn to page 224 now to request more information about ExxonMobil.

ExxonMobil is the world's largest publicly-traded international oil and gas company with a presence in nearly 200 countries and territories. They are a worldwide leader in the petroleum and petrochemicals business.

Exxon Mobil Corporation is the parent company of the Esso, Mobil and ExxonMobil companies in the UK. They operate within a sector that is dynamic, strategically important and exciting. To secure their position within this environment the company strives towards operational excellence with an expert, talented workforce, strong financial resources and cutting-edge technology. Their customers are both global and local, ranging from major airlines to the motorists who buy their engine oils. In the UK they serve around one million customers every day, 365 days of the year, through their 900 service stations and own the country's largest refinery.

A range of exciting career opportunities are available within both commercial and technical functions, where graduates can expect immediate responsibility.

Graduates will receive extensive technical and personal skills training via internal and external courses, as well as through on-the-job training. The graduate programme, run in conjunction with the internationally renowned London Business School (LBS), is a two-year, modular course covering business awareness, interpersonal skills development and people management, and will lead to alumni status with the LBS upon completion of the programme. Obtaining chartership status is also encouraged where appropriate, e.g. IChemE and CIMA.

Rapid skills growth and career development is standard and graduates can expect responsibility from day one, and a high degree of intellectual challenge.

In the next 25 years the demand for energy will increase by as much as 50%.

www.exxonmobil.com/ukrecruitment

It's a challenge like no other.
And it will be solved by someone like you.

The need for energy is a very real economic issue. It affects literally everyone – everywhere in the world. At ExxonMobil, we're uniquely positioned to help find the answers to the world's toughest energy challenges. We have the resources, the technology, and the commitment of people just like you.

When you build your career here, you have the opportunity to make a profound impact. From inventing new technologies, to unlocking new sources of petroleum, to developing more efficient fuel and engine systems, you can make the breakthroughs happen.

The biggest challenges attract the best. Whether your background is in business, engineering, or science, ExxonMobil has a challenging career waiting for you.

ExxonMobil
Taking on the world's toughest energy challenges.

FABER MAUNSELL | AECOM

Vacancies for around
250 graduates in 2008

Consulting

Engineering

Starting salary for 2008
£Competitive

Universities that
Faber Maunsell
plans to visit in 2007-8
Aberdeen, Bath, Belfast,
Birmingham, Bristol,
Cambridge, Cardiff, City,
Durham, Edinburgh,
Exeter, Glasgow,
Heriot-Watt, Lancaster,
Leeds, Leicester,
Liverpool, London,
Loughborough, Manchester,
Newcastle, Nottingham,
Oxford, Plymouth,
Sheffield, Southampton,
Strathclyde, Warwick
Please check with your university
careers service for details of events.

Application deadline
Year-round recruitment

Contact Details
✉ graduates@fabermaunsell.com
☎ 020 8784 5784
Turn to page 224 now to request more
information about Faber Maunsell.

Halley VI Antarctic Research Station

Faber Maunsell is a company that is determined to be different
and to make a difference. Whether delivering a new hospital
for a community, a water infrastructure network for a city or an
integrated transport strategy for an entire region, their team
of engineers, consultants, planners, scientists and managers
deliver the types of projects that underpin all our daily lives.

As part of AECOM, one of the world's largest design and management
companies, their people get the opportunity to work on outstanding projects
across the world. Faber Maunsell is looking for the brightest and best people
to take the company forward. Graduates will be challenged, encouraged and
actively supported towards a relevant professional qualification. Applications
are encouraged from a wide range of disciplines but particularly those with a
degree in a relevant engineering or science-based subject.

Graduate opportunities exist for: civil, structural, building services,
transport and environment engineers; transport and development planners;
environmental scientists, ecologists and other specialists.

Faber Maunsell operates a comprehensive training academy for staff at all
levels, graduate to director, which is designed to help meet specific and
developing training needs. A broad base of structured learning and on-the-job
development gives every new graduate a really strong grounding in his or her
chosen discipline.

Graduates benefit from a £2,000 golden hello, a competitive salary and flexible
benefits giving the opportunity to select a package that suits individual needs,
including help in repaying student loans.

FSA.

Vacancies for around 45 graduates in 2008

Finance

Starting salary for 2008
£28,000

Universities that the Financial Services Authority plans to visit in 2007-8

Aston, Bath, Birmingham, Bristol, Cambridge, Durham, Edinburgh, London, Manchester, Nottingham, Oxford, Sheffield, Warwick, York
Please check with your university careers service for details of events.

Application deadline
5th December 2007

Contact Details
Turn to page 224 now to request more information about the Financial Services Authority.

The role of the Financial Services Authority (FSA) is to help the UK financial services industry work effectively, delivering benefits to firms and consumers alike. From getting a fair deal for everyone in their financial affairs to maintaining London's status as a world-leading international financial centre, the FSA's remit is broad and their influence profound.

Graduates enjoy an unrivalled overview of one of the UK's most complex and critical industries. Setting and monitoring standards for an industry comprising 29,000 financial companies of all sizes; providing key services and information to firms and consumers alike; explaining judgments and decisions to everyone from the media to Parliament: FSA graduates experience it all.

What's more, genuine responsibility is given to graduates from day one of the three year graduate development programme. Three internal rotations and a six-month external secondment provide a unique breadth of insight into the world of financial services. Graduates have previously been seconded to investment banks, law firms, fund managers and professional services firms. All the while, an impressive array of training courses and qualifications ensures ongoing professional and personal development.

By the end of it, FSA graduates are ready to step straight into a long and rewarding career at the heart of the industry – and to make a real difference, both in the City of London and throughout the country.

To find out what it takes to be a financial services authority, and to apply online, visit www.fsa.gov.uk/careers

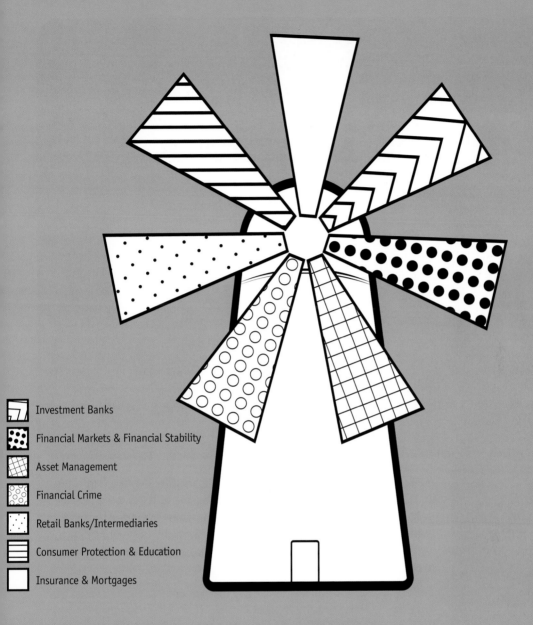

Investment Banks

Financial Markets & Financial Stability

Asset Management

Financial Crime

Retail Banks/Intermediaries

Consumer Protection & Education

Insurance & Mortgages

Three rotations. One unique experience.

Graduate Development Programme

The regulator of the UK financial services industry, the FSA offers a three-year programme that will give you the chance to rotate around three core areas of finance from the list above. Add a six-month external secondment and you'll have a uniquely varied overview of the financial world. Full support will be given to gain professional qualifications.

If you're expecting a 2:1 or above, visit **www.fsa.gov.uk/careers** to find out more and apply. There, you can also find details of our Legal & Finance Development Programmes.

Closing date: 5th December 2007.

THE FINANCIAL SERVICES AUTHORITY

FRESHFIELDS BRUCKHAUS DERINGER

www.freshfields.com/uktrainees

Vacancies for around 100 graduates in 2008
For training contracts starting in 2010

 Law

Starting salary for 2008
£38,000

Universities Freshfields Bruckhaus Deringer plans to visit in 2007-8
Birmingham, Bristol, Cambridge, Cardiff, City, Durham, Edinburgh, Exeter, Glasgow, Kent, Leeds, Leicester, London, Manchester, Newcastle, Northumbria, Nottingham, Oxford, Sheffield, St Andrews, Warwick
Please check with your university careers service for details of events.

Application deadline
31st July 2008

Contact Details
✉ uktrainees@freshfields.com
☎ 020 7427 3194

Turn to page 224 now to request more information about Freshfields Bruckhaus Deringer.

As a leading international law firm with a network of 27 offices in 16 countries, Freshfields provides first-rate legal services to corporations, financial institutions and governments around the world. With clients such as Goldman Sachs, Hewlett Packard, Tesco and the Bank of England, it is recognised as a market leader for a wide range of work.

Trainee solicitors receive a thorough professional training in a very broad range of practice areas, an excellent personal development programme and the chance to work in one of the firm's international offices or on secondment with a client. Flexibility is one of the hallmarks of their training programme and one of the features which most differentiates the Freshfields training contract from others.

The firm has a friendly and relaxed atmosphere which comes from having a diverse range of individuals who share a strong set of common values. A wide range of social, sporting and cultural activities are available and the firm is known for its pro bono work and CSR programme.

There is no such thing as a 'typical' Freshfields lawyer. The firm's broad array of practice areas and clients demands a wide range of individuals with differing skills, abilities and interests. However, successful candidates will need strong academic qualifications (the ability to achieve a high 2.1 or first at degree level), a broad range of skills and a good record of achievement in other areas.

Vacation placements are offered for students in their penultimate year. Please refer to the firm's website for details.

FUJITSU

uk.fujitsu.com/graduates

Vacancies for around 100 graduates in 2008

- Accountancy
- Consulting
- Finance
- Human Resources
- IT
- Marketing
- Purchasing
- Sales

Vacancies also available in Europe.

Starting salary for 2008
£25,000

Universities that Fujitsu plans to visit in 2007-8
Aston, Belfast, Birmingham, Brunel, Cambridge, Cardiff, Edinburgh, Leeds, London, Loughborough, Manchester, Nottingham, Oxford, Reading, Sheffield, Swansea, Warwick
Please check with your university careers service for details of events.

Application deadline
31st January 2008

Contact Details
Turn to page 224 now to request more information about Fujitsu.

The qualities Fujitsu seeks in its graduates are the same qualities their customers seek in them.

The ability to stand out from the crowd, to offer something different and to go that extra mile to achieve success. It's how they've built up a solid reputation. Fujitsu's no-nonsense approach to business and IT means that their customers are many of Europe's leading companies. In addition Fujitsu Services is now number one IT services provider to the UK Government.

Fujitsu is looking for people who will not only enhance their reputation but who have the potential to make a strong contribution to extending and expanding their success. They provide a comprehensive eighteen month development programme to give all graduate entrants the generic business skills required to operate effectively as leaders of the future.

Fujitsu is keen for successful applicants to play an active part in the organisation as quickly as possible. Everything is done to help graduates settle in smoothly. The company has a buddy system that pairs graduates up with someone in their immediate working area, probably a previous graduate, who will be on hand to help with day-to-day issues. Then graduates will have a mentor, an experienced manager, who they meet several times a year to discuss their progression, to understand their strengths and to help plan their career course. Graduates are invited to attend regular events, which offer the chance to compare notes and socialise.

As the European arm of the world's third largest IT company and with revenues in excess of £2.3 billion Fujitsu is securing a long-term future for both their business and their people. For the chance to stand out in an outstanding company apply now.

To be **successful** you have to be **different**.

You could just **follow** the crowd, or **stand out** from them.

What do **you** want to do?

Vacancies for around
200 graduates in 2008

- Accountancy
- Finance
- IT
- Purchasing
- Research & Development

Starting salary for 2008
£24,000

Universities that GCHQ
plans to visit in 2007-8
Please check with your university
careers service for details of events.

Application deadline
Year-round recruitment

Contact Details
✉ recruitment@gchq.gsi.gov.uk

Turn to page 224 now to request
more information about GCHQ.

GCHQ (Government Communications Headquarters) is part
of British Intelligence and works closely with MI5 and MI6 to
counter the threats which face the nation and global community.

Using some of the world's most sophisticated technology, they intercept
communications and electronic signals which teams help turn into intelligence.
Their reports reach the very top of government and can be used to inform
foreign policy decisions, or used in combating terrorism, drugs trafficking, the
proliferation of weapons of mass destruction and international crime.

GCHQ is also charged with preventing hostile forces compromising the UK's
critical communications infrastructure. This is the responsibility of CESG (the
UK National Technical Authority for Information Assurance), a key division
within the business. Together they employ around 4,500 people, mainly at the
HQ in Cheltenham.

Like any large and complex business, a diverse range of people and skills
are needed. While many of these are typical of most organisations (finance,
administration, audit), GCHQ's wider role is unique. And so are the types of
people they recruit. These include IT and telecommunications specialists to
maintain and develop capabilities; linguists to monitor and translate a variety
of communications; mathematicians to help set and crack codes; librarians/
information specialists to provide research; and intelligence analysts to piece
together information.

Everyone benefits from personalised training, support towards professional
qualifications, mentoring and shadowing. GCHQ's campaigns run throughout
the year, please check the website for details. Applicants must be British citizens.

Vacancies for around 200 graduates in 2008

- Accountancy
- Engineering
- Finance
- General Management
- Human Resources
- IT
- Manufacturing
- Marketing
- Sales

Vacancies also available in Europe.

Starting salary for 2008
£Competitive

Universities that GE plans to visit in 2007-8
Aston, Bath, Birmingham, Brunel, City, Lancaster, Leeds, London, Manchester, Nottingham, Warwick
Please check with your university careers service for details of events.

Application deadline
Year-round recruitment

Contact Details
Turn to page 224 now to request more information about GE.

With products and services ranging from aircraft engines, power generation, water processing and security technology to medical imaging, business and consumer financing, media content and industrial products, GE serves customers in more than 100 countries and employs more than 300,000 people worldwide.

GE has been hailed the most admired company of the Fortune 500 for seven out of the last ten years, most recently in 2007. Their global presence, innovation and financial strength help to make GE a dynamic place to work.

Every year GE hires over 1,000 students globally in their renowned Leadership Programmes. At GE graduates are invited to use their imagination and develop a career in finance (FMP), engineering (EEDP), information technology (IMLP), manufacturing (OMLP), sales and marketing (ECLP) or human resources (HRLP).

These programmes combine responsible and important job assignments along with formal classroom studies. The rotational assignments cover different aspects of a GE business, typically involving placements across several European countries, providing successful applicants with broad and valuable experience in a short amount of time.

GE also offers internships allowing students to work side-by-side with experts in the business. They will apply their theoretical knowledge to real-life business problems and develop skills in a cutting-edge global environment. For high-potential interns there is the opportunity to continue working with GE by joining the entry-level leadership program in their chosen field.

Bright ideas welcome.

Every year GE hires over 1,000 students globally into our renowned leadership programs.

Would you like to be one of those?

At GE we invite you to use your imagination through a career in engineering, finance, manufacturing, sales and marketing, human resources, or information technology.

Our leadership programs provide you an unbeatable opportunity to accelerate your career growth. These programs, typically two years in length, are designed to give tremendous breadth of experience and hands-on training. Considered as the talent pipeline for GE's different functional areas, these programs are rotational in nature and combine real work experience with specialized coursework or classroom training.

To learn more visit us at www.gecareers.com/europe
an equal opportunity employer.

GE imagination at work

GlaxoSmithKline

www.gsk.com/uk-students

Vacancies for around 40-50 graduates in 2008

- Accountancy
- Engineering
- Finance
- IT
- Manufacturing
- Marketing
- Purchasing
- Research & Development
- Sales

Starting salary for 2008
£Competitive

Universities that GSK plans to visit in 2007-8
Please check with your university careers service for details of events.

Application deadline
See website for full details.

Contact Details
Turn to page 224 now to request more information about GSK.

GlaxoSmithKline (GSK) is a place where ideas come to life. As one of the world's leading research-based pharmaceutical companies, GSK is dedicated to delivering products and medicines that help millions of people around the world do more, feel better and live longer.

Based in the UK, but with operations in the US and 117 other countries worldwide, GSK make almost 4 billion packs of medicine and healthcare products every year, with sales of £23.2 billion in 2006. And much of this is thanks to an extensive product range that includes everything from prescription medicines to popular consumer healthcare products.

So while some people depend on GSK's pioneering pharmaceutical products to tackle life-threatening illnesses, others choose best-selling nutritional brands such as Lucozade and Ribena for a feel-good boost. GSK even manages to brighten smiles with some of the world's favourite toothpaste brands.

New starters at GSK will soon see that there's no such thing as a typical career path at GSK. With roles at all levels, as well as a number of industrial placements, across all business functions, there are plenty of opportunities to learn and develop.

And with so much geographical and business diversity on offer, GSK is in a great position to give all the support needed. There are no limits on where a career could lead – their various development programmes in the UK have produced some of GSK's most aspiring leaders. Find out more about the opportunities on offer by visiting GSK at www.gsk.com/uk-students

DON'T BLAME US.

Graduate Opportunities: Sales and Marketing, Finance, Science, IT, Purchasing, Regulatory Affairs, Statistics, Engineering and Production Management

When you've turned the page and missed out on the huge variety of roles that are available at GSK, it'll be too late. Too late for us to tell you that in addition to all the exciting scientific opportunities that you'd expect from one of the world's leading research-based pharmaceutical and healthcare companies, there is a wide range of other, non-scientific graduate opportunities you can move into, in areas ranging from IT right through to Marketing. We would offer our sympathy – but you're probably about six or seven pages away by now.

If you are still here though, we imagine you'll be amazed at what's on offer. Visit our website for the most up-to-date opportunities at **www.gsk.com/uk-students**

THE TIMES
GRADUATE RECRUITMENT
AWARDS 2007
'Graduate Employer of Choice'
RESEARCH & DEVELOPMENT

Together we can make life better.

gsk.com/uk-students

Goldman Sachs

www.gs.com/careers

Vacancies for around 250 graduates in 2008

- Accountancy
- Finance
- Human Resources
- Investment Banking
- IT

Vacancies also available in Europe and Asia.

Starting salary for 2008
£Competitive

Universities that Goldman Sachs plans to visit in 2007-8
Please check with your university careers service for details of events.

Application deadline
19th October 2007
See website for full details.

Contact Details
Turn to page 224 now to request more information about Goldman Sachs.

Goldman Sachs is a global investment banking, securities and investment management firm. They provide a wide range of services to a substantial and diversified client base that includes corporations, financial institutions, governments, non-profit organisations and high net worth individuals. In doing so, they bring together people, capital and ideas to make things happen for their clients.

Goldman Sachs welcomes graduates from a wide range of university courses and backgrounds. There are a number of different stages when graduates can consider joining Goldman Sachs. Naturally, these will give different degrees of exposure and responsibility but whether it is as an intern, a new analyst or a new associate, successful applicants will immediately become part of the team with a real and substantial role to play.

Academic discipline is less important than the personal qualities an individual brings with them, however a strong interest in and appreciation of finance is important. Whatever the background, it is intellect, personality and zest for life that the firm values the most.

Goldman Sachs' ability to meet challenges and ensure the firm's success in the future depends on attracting and retaining the highest quality people and the firm makes an unusual effort to identify the best person for every job. They evaluate candidates on six core measures – achievement, leadership, commercial focus, analytical thinking, teamwork and the ability to make an impact. The firm expects commitment, enthusiasm and drive from its employees but in return, offers unparalleled exposure, early responsibility, significant rewards and unlimited career opportunities.

Great minds don't always think alike.

At Goldman Sachs, we welcome people from more than 100 different countries, each with talents as unique as their goals. Here individuality is an asset. You can be, too.

We offer career opportunities for new analysts and associates. To find out more about our career paths and to complete an online application, please visit **www.gs.com/careers**

Google

www.google.com/jobs/students

Vacancies for around 40 graduates in 2008

- Finance
- IT
- Marketing
- Research & Development
- Sales

Vacancies also available in Europe.

Starting salary for 2008
£Competitive

Universities that Google plans to visit in 2007-8
Bristol, Cambridge, Dublin, Edinburgh, London, Manchester, Oxford
Please check with your university careers service for details of events.

Application deadline
30th November 2007
Software Engineering – year-round.

Contact Details
Turn to page 224 now to request more information about Google.

Google's founders built a company around the idea that work should be challenging, and that the challenge should be fun. From their very first days in a Stanford University dorm room, Larry Page and Sergey Brin have focused on creating a unique approach to search and on building an informal atmosphere that breeds an accelerated exchange of ideas.

Believing that "employees are everything", they created a workplace where the main benefit is important projects to which all employees can contribute and from which they can grow. This is an environment where talented, hard-working, fun people are rewarded for their contributions to Google, and for making the world a better place.

One of Google's guiding principles is that "fast is better than slow". Meetings that might take hours elsewhere take place in the queue for lunch. Few walls separate the people who write the code from the people who write the cheques. Serving Google's end-users is at the heart of what they do and is the company's number one priority. To accomplish this, they need people with great aspirations.

Google offers career opportunities to smart, creative individuals who are passionate about making a difference to tens of millions of lives every day. Roles are available in London, at the company's European Headquarters in Dublin, and elsewhere in Europe, and include positions in advertising, client service, marketing, operations, sales and software engineering. More information on all such roles is available at www.google.com/jobs/students

Google is looking for students with great aspirations.

If you've ever imagined being able to use your talent, education and skills to benefit millions of people around the world, Google might be the place for you. Whether you're searching for a fulltime job or an internship, we have opportunities for the brightest minds in many academic disciplines.

One of our goals is to create the most inspiring work environment on the planet - a place where you can dream big and make things happen. If you'd like to be a part of that, we'd love to hear from you.

Check out www.google.com/jobs/students for current openings.

HBOSplc **BANK OF SCOTLAND** **HALIFAX**

Vacancies for around 150 graduates in 2008

- Accountancy
- Finance
- General Management
- Human Resources
- Investment Banking
- IT
- Law
- Marketing
- Retailing
- Sales

Starting salary for 2008
£Competitive

Universities that HBOS plans to visit in 2007-8
Aston, Bath, Belfast,
Birmingham, Bristol,
Cambridge, Cardiff, Durham,
Edinburgh, Glasgow,
Heriot-Watt, Leeds, London,
Manchester, Newcastle,
Nottingham, Sheffield,
St Andrews, Strathclyde,
Warwick, York
Please check with your university careers service for details of events.

Application deadline
See website for full details.

Contact Details
✉ hbosgrads@hodes.co.uk

Turn to page 224 now to request more information about HBOS.

HBOS plc is one of the largest financial services organisations in Europe and is the result of a merger between Bank of Scotland and Halifax plc.

With over 72,000 employees and 22 million customers, HBOS is one of the fastest growing banks in Europe. But behind all the press recording their success, graduates will find a business focused on innovation and dedicated to understanding exactly what everyone from individual customers to large corporations want.

With brands like Halifax, Bank of Scotland, Esure and Intelligent Finance under their umbrella, they combine the resources and market intelligence to create products that make people's lives easier – and help them make some of life's most important financial decisions. Maybe that's why more customers switch to their services every day.

From Project Management and Financial Markets to IT and Corporate Banking, HBOS offers a huge range of graduate opportunities – each one combining on-the-job training with more formal development.

The size of HBOS and the range of schemes means all interests and ambitions can be catered for, so graduates can have a background in anything from maths to marketing, just as long as they are passionate about their work and are ready to take on genuine responsibility. With HBOS continually expanding, successful applicants can rest assured that they will develop just as quickly as the organisation. Most of the schemes require a 2:1 degree, however please visit the website www.hbos-choices.co.uk for specific scheme requirements.

We're the 24th largest company in the world

We're the 21st
largest company
in the world

Graduate Schemes

The 21st largest company in the world, HBOS is the umbrella organisation for some of the most powerful brands in the financial services sector. And that means over 22 million customers trust us to provide them with the best products and services on the market. From credit cards to fund management and insurance to corporate banking, we've assembled the resources and market insights that will drive our growth now and well into the future.

When you join one of our graduate schemes, you'll get an even clearer understanding of just how varied the opportunities we offer really are. Whether your interests are in IT, Financial Markets, HR, General Management or Risk, you'll find we provide the training, development and wide-ranging opportunities that will get your career off to a flying start. And, that's just the beginning.

As part of a company who is getting bigger by the day, you'll be able to progress and grow at exactly the same rate as us. No matter what you're studying, there's every chance you'll find an area of our business that suits you and your ambitions. With a future like ours, the sky really is the limit.

So, if you're ready to share in our success, go to our website for more information and to apply.

www.hbos-choices.co.uk

Getting bigger by the day

Equal opportunities for all - our policy is as simple as that.

   **BANK OF SCOTLAND**   

HSBC ◆X◆

The world's local bank

www.hsbc.com/studentcareers

Vacancies for around 400 graduates in 2008

- Accountancy
- Finance
- General Management
- Investment Banking
- IT
- Logistics
- Retailing
- Sales

Vacancies also available in Europe, Asia, the USA and elsewhere in the world.

Starting salary for 2008
£Competitive

Universities that HSBC plans to visit in 2007-8
Aston, Bangor, Bath, Birmingham, Bristol, Cambridge, Cardiff, City, Durham, Edinburgh, Exeter, Glasgow, Kent, Lancaster, Leeds, Liverpool, London, Loughborough, Manchester, Newcastle, Nottingham, Oxford, Sheffield, Southampton, Warwick
Please check with your university careers service for details of events.

Application deadline
See website for full details.

Contact Details
Turn to page 224 now to request more information about HSBC.

HSBC is one of the largest banking and financial services organisations in the world, with an international network comprising over 10,000 offices in 82 countries and territories in Europe, the Asia-Pacific region, the Americas, the Middle East and Africa.

HSBC provides a wide range of financial services to over 125 million customers in the areas of personal financial services; consumer finance; commercial banking; corporate, investment banking and markets; and private banking.

Exceptional graduates of any discipline are recruited onto their world class training programmes, preparing them for management and executive positions across the business.

These include Commercial Management, Executive Management, Insurance Broking, Information Technology, Retail Management, Corporate Banking, Operations Management, International Management, Investment Banking, Global Markets, Infrastructure, Private Banking, HSBC Investments and HSBC Amanah (Islamic banking).

HSBC also offers a range of internships to promising undergraduates, both in their first year or penultimate year of study.

HSBC is committed to certain key business principles and values. In addition to providing appropriate financial products and following fair, responsible lending policies, HSBC has a strong corporate responsibility programme that contributes to the everyday life of the local communities in which they work. Employees are encouraged to get involved in HSBC's many educational and environmental projects across the globe.

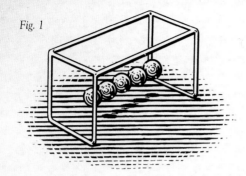

Fig. 1

The Coaster.

A close relation to the sloth,
this is a lesser-spotted creature
which reacts aggressively
to environmental changes.

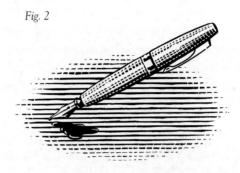

Fig. 2

The Prowler.

A fierce predator willing to hunt
its prey over any distance,
and has even been known to eat
its young in times of drought.

Fig. 3

The Follower.

A domesticated species,
which no longer trusts its instincts.
It is easily panicked
without the security of the herd.

Fig. 4

The Rare Breed.

Highly intelligent and versatile,
it integrates well into any environment.
With strong senses it is the most
switched-on of all species.

HSBC
The world's local bank

If you are a rare breed, please go to **www.hsbc.com/studentcareers**

Vacancies for around 250 graduates in 2008

- Accountancy
- Consulting
- Finance
- IT
- Logistics
- Sales

Starting salary for 2008
£25,000+

Universities that IBM plans to visit in 2007-8
Aston, Bath, Bristol, Brunel, Cambridge, Cardiff, Durham, Edinburgh, Glasgow, Kent, Lancaster, Leeds, Liverpool, London, Loughborough, Manchester, Newcastle, Nottingham, Nottingham Trent, Oxford, Oxford Brookes, Reading, Sheffield, Southampton, Stirling, Strathclyde, Surrey, Warwick, York
Please check with your university careers service for details of events.

Application deadline
Year-round recruitment

Contact Details
✉ graduate@uk.ibm.com

Turn to page 224 now to request more information about IBM.

what makes you * special?

IBM is the world's leading information technology and consulting services company.

Join IBM and see first hand why they were voted the Graduate Employer of the Year and the most popular graduate recruiter in the IT and Communications industry in the 2007 Target National Graduate Recruitment Awards.

With over 90 years of leadership in helping businesses transform, they remain right at the forefront of innovation – topping the US patent list for the 14th year running. Offering complete business solutions, they are a company that is passionate about their clients' success.

IBM has opportunities in IT services, software development, finance and sales, along with opportunities in many areas of consultancy including IT, business, business modelling and supply chain and logistics.

Graduates begin their IBM career with a new hire induction program lasting anything from 3 to 9 weeks. After completion of this, personal, business or technical skills training is provided on an ongoing basis.

IBM is committed to creating an inclusive workplace that embraces diversity. They promote a flexible working environment that sets them apart from their competitors.

IBM are looking for people who want to focus on continuously building their expertise in line with the ever changing business environment. To be considered, graduates should have achieved or be expecting a 2:1 or higher and need to be adaptable, driven, good team players and have a passion for the area of work they are applying to. In return, IBM offers a competitive salary, an excellent flexible benefits package and an environment where talented individuals thrive.

not conventional.

not a follower.

not mainstream.

not just another graduate.

what makes you * special?

* At IBM we've created a special kind of company, the world's most forward looking company, a place that's defined not by what we do today, but what we are going to achieve tomorrow.

And when we look to tomorrow we see creative, innovative graduates, working across all areas of our business – from consultancy to software development, sales to finance – surrounded by opportunities to achieve something special in their careers.

This is what makes us special. We'd like you to think about what makes you special. If you would like to find out more visit **ibm.com/**employment/uk/graduates

IBM welcomes all talent. IBM is focused on recruiting the person with the best skills for each role without regard to race, colour, genetics, religion, gender, gender identity or expression, sexual orientation, national origin, disability or age.

Talent for Innovation | **ibm.com/employment/uk/graduates**

John Lewis

www.jlpjobs.com/graduates

Vacancies for around
20 graduates in 2008

Retailing

Starting salary for 2008
£21,500

Universities John Lewis
plans to visit in 2007-8
Please check with your university
careers service for details of events.

Application deadline
Late November 2007

Contact Details
✉ careers@johnlewis.co.uk

Turn to page 224 now to request
more information about John Lewis.

John Lewis department stores are part of the John Lewis Partnership, one of the best known names in retailing. The John Lewis Partnership occupies a unique position in British retail, it's run by and for the people who work there – the Partners. With the significant number of new store openings planned in the next few years, the opportunities to have a successful management career within John Lewis are on the increase.

The graduate training programme starts with a focus within the department stores, the aim for graduates is to be ready to manage their own selling department in 12-18 months. The responsibilities within this role would include the management of profits, sales upwards of £4 million turnover a year and creating a happy and satisfying work environment for the Partners within the department. Attaining the post of a Department Manager would be the short term focus for graduates who can then progress their careers into senior management positions in-store or in other areas including buying, distribution, merchandising, personnel and finance.

During their training, graduates are supported with both informal and formal development opportunities, including residential courses, seminars and individual coaching and mentoring.

To succeed as a graduate trainee in John Lewis, a passion about working in retail is essential, coupled with the drive to move a graduate career forwards. The ability to deal with a challenging pace of development is paramount, as is commercial awareness and an ability to motivate and inspire.

Ambitious?

Drive a multi-million
pound sales turnover

Lead a team of
more than 30 people

Achieve this within
12–18 months

For more opportunities with the
UK's favourite retailer* visit

jlpjobs.com/graduates

John Lewis

JPMorgan 🔷

Vacancies for around 450 graduates in 2008

- Finance
- Investment Banking
- IT

THIS IS WHERE YOU NEED TO BE.

Starting salary for 2008
£Competitive

Universities JPMorgan plans to visit in 2007-8
Bath, Bristol, Cambridge, Dublin, Durham, Edinburgh, London, Manchester, Nottingham, Oxford, Warwick
Please check with your university careers service for details of events.

Application deadline
18th November 2007

Contact Details
Turn to page 224 now to request more information about JPMorgan.

Graduates will find early responsibility and the chance to make a quick impact at JPMorgan. New technologies, fresh ideas, changing markets and a pipeline of high-quality work all unite to make JPMorgan an exhilarating place to work. There has never been a better time to launch a career with JPMorgan.

JPMorgan is the investment banking business of JPMorgan Chase, a leading global financial services firm with assets of $1.4 trillion and operations in more than 50 countries. The firm serves the interests of clients who have complex financial needs, whether they are major corporations, governments, private firms, financial institutions, non-profit organisations or even private individuals.

The training programmes combine on-the-job learning with classroom instruction that is on par with the world's finest business schools. Graduates will gain exposure to different parts of the business, giving them a multi-dimensional perspective of the company and helping them decide where they might settle. As a result, successful applicants emerge not only with a thorough grounding in their own business area, but also a broad experience of the wider commercial picture and a range of transferable business skills, from project management to team leadership.

JPMorgan is looking for team players and future leaders with exceptional drive, creativity and interpersonal skills. Impeccable academic credentials are important, but so are achievements outside the classroom. More information and helpful advice about graduate careers and internship opportunities can be found at jpmorgan.com/careers

JPMorgan

IT'S YOUR TIME.

We've spent about 200 years getting ready for you. We've built an investment bank that does bigger, more complex deals than anyone else; changed perceptions in everything from technology development to winning women; created a robust global business platform and nurtured a strong, supportive team spirit. Now we're entering the most exciting stage of our history. If you've never considered a career in investment banking before, you should now. Whatever you want from the future – intellectual challenge, fast-track development, recognition, fulfilment, a richer life, or all of the above – **This is where you need to be.**

jpmorgan.com/careers

**Vacancies for around
1,000 graduates in 2008**

- Accountancy
- Finance
- Human Resources
- IT
- Marketing
- Sales

Vacancies also available in Europe.

Starting salary for 2008
£Competitive

Universities that KPMG plans to visit in 2007-8
Aberdeen, Aston, Bath, Birmingham, Bristol, Cambridge, Cardiff, City, Durham, Edinburgh, Exeter, Glasgow, Lancaster, Leeds, Liverpool, London, Loughborough, Manchester, Newcastle, Nottingham, Oxford, Reading, Sheffield, Southampton, St Andrews, Strathclyde, Warwick, York
Please check with your university careers service for details of events.

Application deadline
Year-round recruitment

Contact Details

✉ ukfmgraduate@kpmg.co.uk

Turn to page 224 now to request more information about KPMG.

KPMG is part of an international network of business advisers with almost 100,000 people across their global network in nearly 150 countries. In the UK, they have over 10,000 partners and staff and provide clients with audit, tax and advisory services from more than 20 offices.

KPMG in the UK is also one of the leading employers of graduates, and offers a wide range of high-quality, challenging careers to people from every academic discipline. There are over 20 different graduate career routes to choose from within KPMG, each of which offers a great balance of structured support and real business challenge. Many of their graduate careers also lead to highly respected and valuable professional qualifications.

KPMG has recently been named in the top three 'Best Big Companies To Work For' by The Sunday Times for the third year in a row and voted 'Employer Of The Year' by Accountancy Age. The CBI also named the firm 'Big Four Auditor of the Year' for the third year running.

Just as importantly, KPMG also maintained their track record of consistently exceeding national institutes' average pass rates – a testament to both the high-calibre people they recruit and the extensive support they provide at every stage.

This is an exciting and dynamic time to join KPMG. The merger of the UK firm with member firms in Europe to create KPMG Europe will make it the largest accountancy firm in Europe – capable not only of meeting the needs of the firm's increasingly global clients, but also giving a range of international challenges and opportunities to the firm's talented people.

We don't promise our graduates the Earth.

Just Europe.

Graduate careers, all disciplines

We're not the sort of employer to make wild claims, but we have to admit to being genuinely excited about recent developments in our business – and what they could mean for you. The merger of our UK firm with other KPMG European practices to create KPMG Europe will make us the largest accountancy firm in Europe. For clients, it will mean enhanced capabilities across our audit, tax and advisory areas. And for the most ambitious and talented graduates, it will make us uniquely positioned among our competitors to offer exciting careers on the international stage.

Want to be a part of it?
Visit **www.kpmg.co.uk/careers** to find out how.

AUDIT ▪ TAX ▪ ADVISORY

WORLD LEADER IN BEAUTY PRODUCTS

**Vacancies for around
30 graduates in 2008**

- Engineering
- Logistics
- Marketing
- Sales

Starting salary for 2008
£27,000+

**Universities that L'Oréal
plans to visit in 2007-8**
Bath, Cambridge,
Dublin, London,
Manchester, Nottingham,
Nottingham Trent, Oxford
Please check with your university
careers service for details of events.

Application deadline
Year-round recruitment

Contact Details
Turn to page 224 now to request
more information about L'Oréal.

With more than 130 products sold per second worldwide, L'Oréal is the global leader in cosmetics. L'Oréal's brand portfolio includes some of the world's most recognised beauty and fragrance brands: L'Oréal Paris, Lancôme, Kérastase, Ralph Lauren, Garnier, Biotherm, Maybelline and Body Shop.

With 60,851 people employed in over 58 countries and 19 global brands sold in more than 130 nations, L'Oréal is a committed Investor in People.

The company is looking to recruit entrepreneurs with a creative flair who want to be challenged and are willing to take on responsibilities from day one.

Each year L'Oréal offers 30 graduate management trainees the opportunity to join a year-long, individually tailor-made programme providing three on-the-job placements in different business areas. At L'Oréal graduates work across diverse functions: marketing, sales, PR, market research, visual merchandising, logistics or HR in order to get a 360° exposure to the company's business.

At L'Oréal graduates are encouraged to excel and are guided at every step. They receive expert training on topics related to professional development, business knowledge and personal impact. At L'Oréal, graduates are nurtured to become future general managers of the company and lead a career of international scope.

The company's stimulating, motivating, open-minded and dynamic culture is a catalyst in making L'Oréal the No. 1 FMCG employer of choice.

Learning for development, dedicated mentors, flexible working environment and the company's invigorating and energetic culture lead to graduates pursuing international fast-track careers.

TO BUILD BEAUTY, WE NEED TALENT.

"BEAUTY IS MY BUSINESS. AND BUSINESS IS MY PASSION FOR CREATIVITY AND ENTREPRENEURSHIP."

Martin M.

MARKETING DIRECTOR, L'ORÉAL COLUMBIA

FAST-TRACK CAREERS
INTERNATIONAL OPPORTUNITIES
INDIVIDUAL DEVELOPMENT PROGRAMMES

L'ORÉAL
WORLD LEADER IN BEAUTY PRODUCTS

THE NUMBER ONE BEAUTY COMPANY IN THE WORLD IS ON THE HUNT FOR DYNAMIC, CAPABLE, INNOVATIVE AND RESULTS-DRIVEN STUDENTS WHO ASPIRE TO A JET-SET, FAST-PACED CAREER.

FROM MONITORING THE SUCCESS OF MEN EXPERT IN THE UK, TO MANAGING THE MULTI-MILLION BRAND PORTFOLIO OF GIORGIO ARMANI FRAGRANCES IN SYDNEY, FROM FORECASTING THE GROWTH POTENTIAL OF VICHY'S INGENIOUS NEW CREAM IN HONG KONG TO DEVISING A LAUNCH PLAN FOR REDKEN'S LATEST STYLING PRODUCTS IN NEW YORK – PEOPLE WHO HAVE JOINED US HAVE BUILT THEIR CAREERS TO INTERNATIONAL ACCLAIM.

JOIN US FOR A COMPLETE GLOBAL BUSINESS ADVENTURE.

FOR MORE INFORMATION ON OUR TAILOR-MADE GRADUATE PROGRAMME IN MARKETING, SALES, SUPPLY CHAIN AND ENGINEERING LOG ONTO: WWW.LOREALBUSINESSCLASS.CO.UK

Linklaters

www.linklaters.com/careers/ukgrads

Vacancies for around 130 graduates in 2008

For training contracts starting in September 2010/March 2011

Law

Starting salary for 2008
£36,000

Universities Linklaters plans to visit in 2007-8

Birmingham, Bristol, Cambridge, Dublin, Durham, Edinburgh, Exeter, Leeds, Leicester, London, Manchester, Nottingham, Oxford, Sheffield, Southampton, St Andrews, Warwick

Please check with your university careers service for details of events.

Application deadline
See website for full details.

Contact Details

✉ graduate.recruitment@linklaters.com

Turn to page 224 now to request more information about Linklaters.

Linklaters LLP is the global law firm that advises the world's leading companies, financial institutions and governments on their most challenging transactions and assignments. This is an ambitious and innovative firm: the drive to create something new in professional services also shapes a very special offer to graduates.

The firm recruits graduates from both law and non-law disciplines. Non-law graduates spend a conversion year at law school taking the Graduate Diploma in Law (GDL). All trainees have to complete the Legal Practice Course (LPC) before starting their training contracts. The firm meets the costs of both the GDL and LPC and provides a maintenance grant for both.

While many law firms have strengths in particular areas, Linklaters is strong across the full range of commercial, corporate and financial law; this makes the firm an especially stimulating place to train as a business lawyer. The training contract is built around four six-month seats or placements in a range of practice areas. This develops well-rounded lawyers, but it also helps trainees plan their careers after qualifying.

Linklaters people come from many different backgrounds and cultures; by working together to achieve great things for clients, they are encouraged to achieve their own ambitions and potential. Training with Linklaters means working alongside some of the world's best lawyers on some of the world's most challenging deals. The firm expects a lot of its trainees, but the rewards – personal and professional as well as financial – are very high indeed.

'So
what's it really like?'

How is it, such a simple question can so
often be avoided by employers? It's the
one thing you probably want to ask – and
definitely need to know. On our website
we've included various features that are
designed to give an honest flavour of
Linklaters. There's really no substitute for
the kind of exposure you get on a vacation
scheme or by meeting people at campus
events, but we've done our best to provide
insights and information that come a
close second. We hope you'll visit soon.

What do you need to know?
www.linklaters.com/careers/ukgrads

Linklaters LLP

Linklaters

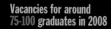 **Lloyds TSB** | for the journey...

Vacancies for around 75-100 graduates in 2008

- Accountancy
- Finance
- General Management
- Human Resources
- Investment Banking
- IT
- Marketing
- Retailing
- Sales

Starting salary for 2008
£25,000-£33,450

Universities Lloyds TSB plans to visit in 2007-8
Aston, Bath, Birmingham, Bristol, Cardiff, Edinburgh, Exeter, Lancaster, Leeds, Liverpool, Manchester, Newcastle, Nottingham, Reading, Sheffield, Southampton, St Andrews, Strathclyde, Warwick
Please check with your university careers service for details of events.

Application deadline
See website for full details.

Contact Details
✉ graduates@lloydstsb.co.uk
☎ 01903 844942
Turn to page 224 now to request more information about Lloyds TSB.

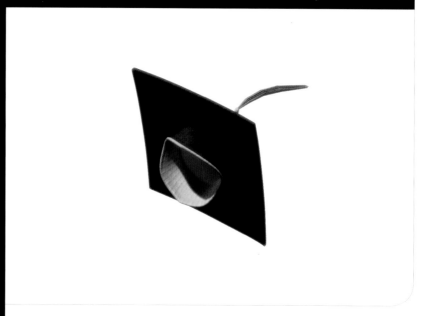

Whatever graduates want from their career, Lloyds TSB is there every step of the way with on-going support and development opportunity.

Though Lloyds TSB is one of the UK's most popular banks, there's far more to their business than just a network of high-street branches. One of the world's leading financial services companies, with Scottish Widows and Cheltenham & Gloucester in their portfolio, they're a major international group with a presence in 20 countries and some 80,000 employees. All of which means there's no shortage of career destinations.

Graduates start out on one of their management programmes – in finance, IT leadership or general management. From there, successful applicants find themselves on year-long tailor-made placements across the business, each designed to build up skills and leadership qualities.

Supported with formal and informal training, graduates will develop confidence and credibility, preparing them for a future leadership role in one of their core areas: people management, strategy, relationship management or operations.

Lloyds TSB understands how people's needs evolve over time – and that's no different with careers. A graduate might start out with a particular path in mind – but things can change along the way. That's why Lloyds TSB is looking for people with an open and inquisitive mind and the willingness to learn, develop and change. That way, they will get the most out of the programme and their potential – and from the wider Lloyds TSB business. But graduates can be sure that wherever they end up, it will be another new beginning.

From learning to earning, we'll help you all the way.

Graduate Programme

- Corporate Markets • Finance
- Audit • IT • HR • Marketing
- Internships • Industrial Placements
- Business Specialist Programme

On our Management Training Programmes, the step from university to work can be rewarding – and not just because of our highly attractive salaries. With the opportunity to shape your own career path every bit as much as we'll help shape you, we certainly won't make up our minds about you in advance. Instead, we'll encourage you to set your own course, and make up your own mind about your future. All we ask is that you're a creative and independent thinker with excellent academic credentials, and that you're ready for anything, willing to learn and determined to do well.

To find out more and apply online please visit
www.lloydstsbtalent.co.uk

CIMA
TRAINING QUALITY PARTNER

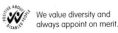

We value diversity and always appoint on merit.

Lovells

www.lovells.com/graduates

**Vacancies for around
90 graduates in 2008**
For training contracts starting in 2010

 Law

Starting salary for 2008
£36,000

**Universities that Lovells
plans to visit in 2007-8**
Birmingham, Bristol,
Cambridge, Cardiff, City,
Durham, East Anglia,
Edinburgh, Exeter, Leeds,
Leicester, Liverpool,
London, Manchester,
Newcastle, Nottingham,
Oxford, Reading, Sheffield,
St Andrews, Warwick, York
Please check with your university
careers service for details of events.

Application deadline
See website for full details.

Contact Details
✉ recruit@lovells.com

Turn to page 224 now to request
more information about Lovells.

Lovells is an international legal practice comprising Lovells LLP
and its affiliated businesses. Lovells has offices in the major
financial and commercial centres across Europe, Asia and
the USA.

Lovells' international strength across a wide range of practice areas gives them
an exceptional reputation not only for corporate, finance and dispute resolution
but also for other specialist areas including intellectual property, employment,
EU/competition, insurance and tax.

High calibre candidates, who are interested in applying, should be able to
demonstrate strong academic/intellectual ability, ambition, strong commercial
skills and interpersonal skills, and a professional/commercial attitude.

A trainee at Lovells spends six months in four different areas of the practice to
gain as much experience as possible. They have the option of spending time
in their second year of training in an international office or on secondment to
the in-house legal department of a major client. A comprehensive programme
of skills training is run for trainees both in-house and externally that comprises
the Professional Skills Course. Trainees are offered as much responsibility as
they can handle as well as regular reviews, six-month appraisals and support.
After qualification, training and professional development remain a priority.

Lovells offer up to 90 vacation placements over four highly regarded schemes
lasting two or three weeks at Christmas, Easter and over the summer. Places
are principally offered to penultimate-year law, and final year non-law students,
but graduates and individuals considering a change of career are also
welcome to apply.

One firm, eight time zones.

Can you handle the pace?

Lovells

MAERSK

**Vacancies for around
15-20 graduates in 2008**

Finance

General Management

Human Resources

Starting salary for 2008
£Competitive

**Universities that Maersk
plans to visit in 2007-8**
Bath, Birmingham, Bristol,
Cambridge, Cardiff,
Durham, Edinburgh,
London, Nottingham
Please check with your university
careers service for details of events.

Application deadline
30th April 2008

Contact Details
Turn to page 224 now to request
more information about Maersk.

As one of the world's leading transportation businesses, the
A.P. Moller – Maersk Group is a truly international business.
Their people are from every corner of the globe and with offices
in 125 countries, their operations span it. As such a career with
Maersk will literally put the world at a graduate's fingertips.

Lasting two years, their graduate programmes will set on an international
path to senior leadership in the organisation. On both of the two streams,
Business or Finance, graduates will initially learn the fundamentals of the
business before progressing, through a series of placements, to gain a
more strategic perspective.

On the Business stream, they offer placements in the core areas of the
organisation including: Global Operations; Supply Chain Management; Trade
and Ship Owning. The Finance stream placements will expose successful
applicants to the varying financial operations of their different business units
and corporate functions. They'll also offer support in attaining a professional
qualification (ACCA or CIMA).

Whichever stream graduates join, they'll work towards an industry recognised
internal diploma at Maersk's training centre in Copenhagen. Here graduates
will learn the ins and outs of the industry and enhance understanding of their
global operations. Juggling work and study isn't easy though. It demands a
strong commitment and a willingness to invest the necessary time and effort.
However, the rewards are worth it. On graduating from the UK scheme,
graduates will put that global knowledge into practice with a two year role in
one of their offices in over 125 countries across the world.

Set off on a voyage of discovery

International Careers in Business and Finance

At Maersk, we have a simple proposition; give us two years and we'll give you a whole world of opportunities. As a leading global shipping and logistics business, we are a truly international organisation, operating throughout the world 24 hours a day, 7 days a week. As you might expect, our graduate programmes in Business or Finance don't just give you a thorough understanding of our industry, they also provide you with the skills you'll need on your international route to senior management in our organisation. In fact, on completion of one of our UK graduate programmes you'll take your first step on this voyage: a challenging role in one of our offices in over 125 countries worldwide. To see where we could take you, visit www.maersk.co.uk/recruitment

MAERSK

YOUR M&S

www.marksandspencer.com/gradcareeers

Vacancies for around 100 graduates in 2008

- Human Resources
- IT
- Purchasing
- Retailing

Starting salary for 2008
£22,000-£25,500

Universities that Marks & Spencer plans to visit in 2007-8
Aston, Bath, Cambridge, Cardiff, Durham, Edinburgh, Leeds, Leicester, Liverpool, Loughborough, Manchester, Nottingham, Oxford, Southampton, Surrey, Warwick, York
Please check with your university careers service for details of events.

Application deadline
December 2007

Contact Details
Turn to page 224 now to request more information about Marks & Spencer.

When it comes to offering graduates a thorough grounding in retail, the Marks & Spencer scheme is hard to beat.

The scheme involves taking on three or four placements over the course of around 12 months. Alongside this on-the-job training, graduates receive classroom tuition, designed to help them develop expert knowledge, as well as personal skills in areas such as negotiation and leadership. By the end of the scheme, they should have everything they need to take on their first big management role. That could mean leading a team of people or running an area of the business worth millions of pounds. In all likelihood, it will mean both.

Most M&S graduates join them in a store-based role, and are placed on a fast-track route into senior level retail management. If everything goes as planned, then this will mean running a small store – or a whole department of a large one – after about a year.

Alternatively, they can join an 18-month store-based HR programme. This route offers the chance to develop specialist skills and expertise, gain professional qualifications, and build a successful, long-term HR career.

There are also places available in a range of head office areas, including IT, buying and merchandising, garment and food technology, as well as opportunities for undergraduates to do 12-month business placements.

M&S aren't just looking for any graduates. They're looking for the best around. People with the drive and ambition to make the most of all the opportunities on offer. And people who can match the energy, vision and ideas that have kept M&S at the forefront of their industry for so long.

This is not just any graduate scheme.

MARS
incorporated

www.mars.com/ultimategrads

Vacancies for around 30+ graduates in 2008

- Engineering
- Finance
- General Management
- Marketing
- Research & Development
- Sales

Starting salary for 2008
£29,000
Plus bonus.

Universities that Mars plans to visit in 2007-8
Bath, Bristol, Cambridge, Edinburgh, Leeds, Manchester, Nottingham, Oxford, Warwick
Please check with your university careers service for details of events.

Application deadline
18th November 2007
See website for full details.

Contact Details
✉ mars.graduate@eu.effem.com

Turn to page 224 now to request more information about Mars.

Enjoy

that

feeling of

inevitable

success.

Mars®, Uncle Ben's®, Snickers®, Whiskas®, M&M's®, Dolmio®, Twix®, Pedigree®, Maltesers®... these are just some of the household name brands that form the global, $21bn Mars portfolio. It's little wonder then that it takes 30,000 associates on 140 sites in 60 countries to run a business on this scale. It will also come as no surprise that when recruiting graduates, Mars settles for the very highest calibre.

Surprisingly, Mars Incorporated is still a private, family-owned business. They invest only their own profits in developing the organisation. This means that their graduates – razor sharp business-leaders-in-the-making – get to take more educated risks, explore more avenues and achieve more of everything.

Mars offers development programmes for those who want to specialise in finance, marketing, sales, engineering or R&D. These programmes allow graduates to expand their knowledge, stretch their talent and discover a wealth of new skills. Graduates will have access to Mars' tailored training curriculum covering topics such as presentation, leadership and people management skills. Mars also supports all its graduates to achieve professional qualifications with financial sponsorship and study leave.

If that wasn't enough, there's the grand prix of graduate schemes – the Mars Management Development Programme. This is a three-year fast-track for the best graduate talent, the opportunity to gain unparalleled experience across all areas of the business, and a platform for a career with no limits.

With outstanding development programmes to choose from, world-class brands to work with, an impressive peer group to grow alongside and commercial legends to follow, how could it be any other way? Visit www.mars.com/ultimategrads for more.

Choose carefully,

because there's no
going back to obscurity.

i'm lovin' it

**Vacancies for around
150 graduates in 2008**

■ General Management
■ Retailing

Starting salary for 2008
£18,500-£21,500

**Universities McDonald's
plans to visit in 2007-8**
Please check with your university
careers service for details of events.

Application deadline
Year-round recruitment

Contact Details
✉ managementrecruitment@
uk.mcd.com
☎ 020 8700 7007

Turn to page 224 now to request
more information about McDonald's.

Forget the myth that says McDonald's only offers McJobs.
The reality is very different – and far more interesting.
McDonald's management careers offer exceptional challenge
and support, some excellent rewards and all the potential of a
world-famous brand.

Their 20-week management development programme prepares graduates
for running a restaurant – Business Management as they call it. This is
commercial management in its fullest sense. Graduates gain valuable
operational experience in the restaurants, and, as importantly, benefit from
wide-ranging commercial exposure. They cover everything from leadership
and people development to cash control and profit maximisation.

Provided they excel on the programme, within a few years of joining graduates
could be managing a £million business with a 60-strong team: a McDonald's
restaurant. After that they join a management career path that could lead to
Executive team level. Naturally, not everyone will climb that high. But as long
as they have leadership potential and can make the most of the award-winning
training, there's no reason why graduates shouldn't set their sights high.

McDonald's urges graduates to do some soul-searching before applying.
McDonald's managers set the tone of their restaurants, bringing the best
out of their team. To build their businesses, they have to display energy,
commitment and hard work every day. And they need to combine both
decisiveness and sensitivity; ideas and action. Only by blending all these
qualities will graduates excel on one of the most stimulating management
development programmes around.

Mc**Prospects**

Over half our Executive Team started in our restaurants.
Not bad for a Mc**Job**

Start your McDonald's career as a **Trainee Business Manager** and where you end up is entirely up to you. There are no limits on how far or how fast you progress. You could be running your own £million restaurant within a few years of joining us. Then beyond that is a career path that stretches all the way to our Executive Team. Of course, not everyone will climb to this level. But with our award-winning management training and your gifts for leadership and business, why shouldn't you set your sights high?
Apply online at **www.mcdonalds.co.uk/careers** or call our **Recruitment Hotline on 020 8700 7007.**

i'm lovin' it

McKinsey&Company

www.mckinsey.co.uk

Vacancies for no fixed quota **of graduates in 2008**

■ Consulting

Vacancies also available in Europe, the USA, Asia and elsewhere in the world.

Starting salary for 2008
£Competitive

Universities that McKinsey & Company plans to visit in 2007-8

Bath, Bristol, Cambridge, Dublin, Durham, Edinburgh, Glasgow, Heriot-Watt, London, Nottingham, Oxford, St Andrews, Strathclyde, Warwick, York
Please check with your university careers service for details of events.

Application deadline
Year-round recruitment

Contact Details
✉ london_opportunities@ mckinsey.com
☎ 0207 961 7070

Turn to page 224 now to request more information about McKinsey & Company.

McKinsey & Company is a place where recent graduates can have immediate and direct contact with some of the world's top CEOs and public leaders and where their opinions are encouraged and valued.

As a leading global management consultancy, McKinsey's goal is to provide distinctive and long-lasting performance improvements to their clients, who range from governments and multinationals to charities and entrepreneurial firms.

McKinsey believes that bright, highly motivated newcomers to the business world can bring fresh and innovative insights to bear on their clients' problems. Each year, McKinsey hires a number of outstanding graduates and Masters students from a diverse range of academic disciplines as business analysts.

As business analysts, graduates work as part of a small team consisting of clients and McKinsey colleagues from around the world. Dedicated to one project at a time, they contribute fully: gathering and analysing data, interviewing, coaching and listening, making recommendations and presenting these findings to clients. McKinsey's work cuts across every business sector; from multimedia to energy, banking to retail, and e-commerce to healthcare.

Business analysts are supported with day to day mentoring and coaching, coupled with comprehensive formal training programmes from day one, in order to develop their full potential. McKinsey's commitment to development begins prior to joining with funding for overseas language tuition and training in business basics. McKinsey provides invaluable skills, hands-on experience and a thorough grounding in the commercial world.

greater
expectations

We welcome applications from all degree
disciplines. To find out more please visit
www.mckinsey.co.uk

McKinsey&Company

MERCER

www.mercer.com/ukgrads

**Vacancies for around
80 graduates in 2008**

■ Consulting

■ Finance

Starting salary for 2008
£Competitive

**Universities that Mercer
plans to visit in 2007-8**
Aston, Bath, Belfast,
Birmingham, Bristol,
Cambridge, Cardiff,
City, Durham, Edinburgh,
Exeter, Glasgow,
Heriot-Watt, Hull, Lancaster,
Leeds, Liverpool, London,
Loughborough, Manchester,
Newcastle, Nottingham,
Oxford, Reading, Sheffield,
St Andrews, Stirling,
Strathclyde, Surrey, Sussex,
Warwick, York
Please check with your university
careers service for details of events.

Application deadline
Year-round recruitment

Contact Details
✉ graduates@mercer.com
☎ 0845 600 2389

Turn to page 224 now to request
more information about Mercer.

Mercer is the world's largest human resource and employee benefits consultancy with around 13,000 employees operating in over 40 countries. The solutions they offer their clients include examining the best way to reward their top executives, investigating the intricacies of a company's pension scheme and providing stock market investment advice. They currently advise over 60% of the FTSE 100 companies and many of the Global Fortune 500.

Graduates can join their retirement business as an actuarial trainee and support a variety of actuarial and consultancy projects. Alternatively, they can become retirement analysts and support other Mercer businesses with a variety of valuation data and liability calculations. It could be that a graduate's skills lie in pensions consultancy as a trainee, helping to deliver packaged pension and employee benefits solutions. Or they can join as an investment consultant, providing advice to Mercer's clients on the methods for structuring and investing their assets. As well as undergoing an excellent graduate development programme, most routes will lead to a professional qualification.

Candidates need at least 300 UCAS points and an expected 2:1 honours degree (2:2 for the valuation analysts role) in any discipline. Actuarial Trainees must also have A level Mathematics at grade B or above.

Mercer are looking for graduates who enjoy the challenge of delivering results under tight deadlines. Above all, they want graduates who are keen to build their skills, and add value to Mercer in a truly world-class marketplace.

MERCER

You'll get inspirational job, after influential job, after complex job

Alongside some of the finest financial and numerical talents in the country

Actuaries, Analysts and Consultants based across the UK

You might be flattered to hear that Mercer, one of the largest consultancies of its kind in the world, has more than one role in mind for you. You see, while you might have learnt enough to get 300 UCAS points and at least a 2:1 in a numerical or business-related degree, you probably still don't quite know how far your professional abilities could take you.

Yes, inspirational challenges involving big numbers and some of the UK's most influential businesses are important (we billed $1.5 billion last year, and count 60% of the FTSE100 among our clients). And you'll certainly want colleagues whose expertise you can lean on, learn from and add to in equal measure. But as to what you'll do in five or ten years' time? Well, prove you can deliver first class retirement, employee benefits and investment solutions to our clients, helping release the power of their people, and we'll give you challenges varied enough for an entire career. Go where your strengths lie, visit **www.mercer.com/ukgrads**

We're committed to building a business full of diverse talent, skill and experience.

www.mercer.com

INVESTOR IN PEOPLE

Merrill Lynch

ml.com/careers/europe

**Vacancies for around
450 graduates in 2008**

- Finance
- Human Resources
- Investment Banking
- IT
- Research & Development

Vacancies also available in Europe.

Starting salary for 2008
£Competitive

**Universities Merrill Lynch
plans to visit in 2007-8**

Bristol, Cambridge,
Durham, Glasgow, London,
Manchester, Nottingham,
Oxford, Reading,
Southampton, St Andrews,
Warwick, York

Please check with your university
careers service for details of events.

Application deadline
See website for full details.

Contact Details

Turn to page 224 now to request more
information about Merrill Lynch.

Merrill Lynch is a leading wealth management, capital markets and advisory company with offices on six continents. They have full-time and internship programmes in the following areas: Global Markets, Global Investment Banking, Global Private Client, Research, Technology and Human Resources.

Upon joining one of their programmes, potential applicants will start in New York with an intensive induction. This introduction will also allow the opportunity to meet, work and socialise with other new analysts from around the world.

On return to the local office, graduates will get to grips with professional projects, whilst Merrill Lynch provides a grounding in all of the tools, techniques and work practices needed to succeed.

Merrill Lynch offers penultimate year students the opportunity to gain an insight into the organisation through their nine-week summer programme. This is an opportunity to meet management, analysts and other interns through a range of networking activities.

Prior to the penultimate year, students can also compete with a team of colleagues from university by taking the Merrill Lynch Challenge. The finalist teams participate in a one-week programme in London during the spring.

Ambitious, confident and highly motivated, potential applicants will be natural team players with a desire for a future in financial services. Whatever the academic background, graduates will have an inquiring mind with the ability to communicate complex messages in a clear, simple way. Relevant work experience and foreign languages are also an advantage.

global reputation

[limitless potential]

growth and success

inspiring colleagues

Merrill Lynch is one of the world's leading wealth management, capital markets and advisory companies. Our iconic brand and global capabilities offer you the chance to realise your potential whilst working side-by-side with thought leaders on projects of breathtaking scope and complexity. Join us and you can also benefit from a performance-based culture of excellence, where respect for the individual, commitment to breakthrough, big-picture thinking and enduring values create an environment for your continued growth and success.

For more information or to apply online, visit

ml.com/careers/europe

Merrill Lynch is an equal opportunity employer.

THE SUNDAY TIMES
100
BEST COMPANIES TO WORK FOR · 2007

ml.com/careers/europe

Merrill Lynch

METROPOLITAN POLICE

Working together for a safer London

www.metpolicecareers.co.uk

Vacancies for around
TBC graduates in 2008

☐ Other

Starting salary for 2008
£29,847
On completion of initial
31 weeks' training.

Universities that the Met plans to visit in 2007-8
Please check with your university careers service for details of events.

Application deadline
Year-round recruitment

Contact Details
Turn to page 224 now to request more information about the Met.

The Metropolitan Police Service is always growing and evolving to meet the ever-changing demands of London's vibrant mix of nationalities, faiths and cultures. The dedication to finding new ways to provide the kind of service that London wants and needs has seen the organisation recognised on a global scale as a leading authority on policing today.

Founded in 1829 by Home Secretary Sir Robert Peel, the Met started out with just 1,000 officers policing a population of 2 million. Fast-forward to the 21st century and there are now some 50,000 officers and staff responsible for 7.2 million Londoners, spanning 32 boroughs and 620 square miles.

As London's biggest employer, Met people come from all walks of life, have all manner of skills and experiences and carry out all sorts of different roles. As well as the officers out on the policing frontline, the Met also employs 14,000 members of police staff who are involved in everything from answering emergency calls to training horses, keeping their accounts in order to working at the cutting-edge of IT.

Because the Met is committed to creating a police service that fully reflects London's diversity, it's essential that all applicants have a genuine respect and sensitivity for working effectively with the capital's many different communities.

The sheer size and diversity of the Met brings unique challenges but it also brings unique rewards. Benefits include good salaries, excellent career prospects, a superb pension and the unparalleled sense of pride that comes with helping to make London safer.

WILL YOUR DEGREE MAKE THINGS ANY BETTER?

You can't use your degree certificate as a tissue to wipe away the tears. Neither can you use it as a sticking plaster to patch up the past. But it can still make seven million Londoners feel safe.

We won't treat you any differently just because you're a graduate. Instead, we'll take what you've learnt, move it out of the examination hall and apply it to the real world. Then it's up to you.

Discover what your qualifications really qualify you for. Seven million Londoners are depending on it.

Find out how much by going to
www.metpolicecareers.co.uk

We particularly welcome applications from students from under-represented communities.

SECURITYSERVICE
MI5

Vacancies for around TBC graduates in 2008

- Engineering
- Finance
- Human Resources
- IT

Starting salary for 2008
£Varies by function
See website for full details.

Universities that MI5 plans to visit in 2007-8
Please check with your university careers service for details of events.

Application deadline
Year-round recruitment

MI5 is the UK's security intelligence agency. Through the collection, dissemination and analysis of intelligence MI5 protects the nation's people, economy and institutions from threats such as terrorism and espionage. To do this takes talented people from a range of backgrounds.

MI5 offers a range of careers. So whatever degree graduates might have it is likely there is a role that suits their skills and abilities. MI5 also looks for a strong range of personal qualities.

Many graduates join as intelligence officers. This demanding and rewarding role involves assessing or investigating threats to national security. Most intelligence officers move departments every 18 months to three years so as well as investigative work a career could include policy, personnel, finance or operational work. Intelligence officers have their own areas of responsibility but work as part of a team.

There are also career opportunities as administrative assistants, electronic technicians, English language transcribers, working in our language unit, mobile surveillance officers and IT roles.

As well as vital and varied work, there are lots of other benefits. Training and development programmes give a broader understanding of the organisation and equip staff with the specialist skills needed to make the most of the career opportunities available. The salary and rewards are competitive and include a generous pension scheme and holiday entitlement. Graduates joining the organisation can look forward to working with people from a range of backgrounds in a friendly, team-orientated working environment with a strong sense of camaraderie.

Contact Details
Turn to page 224 now to request more information about MI5.

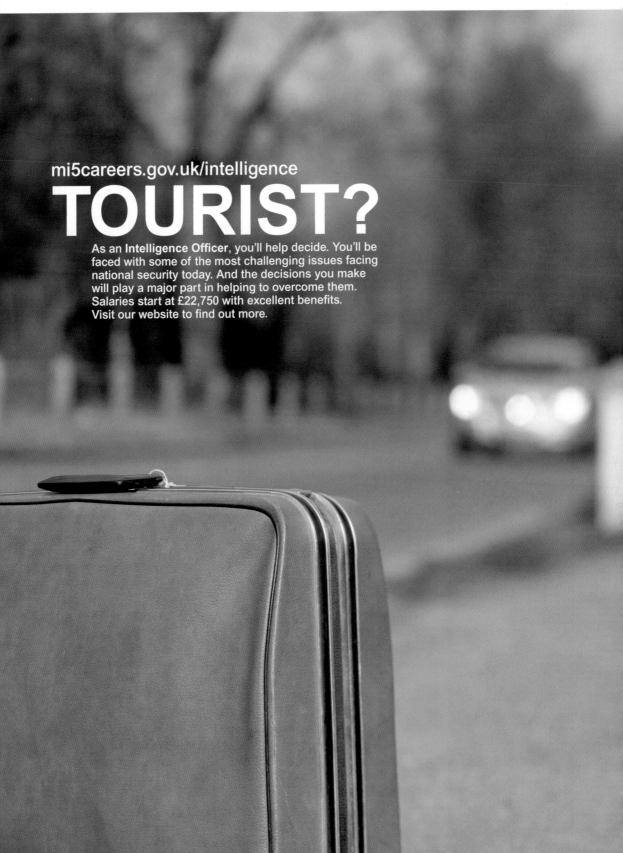

Microsoft®

Your potential. Our passion.™

Vacancies for around 30 graduates in 2008

- IT
- Marketing
- Sales

Starting salary for 2008
£26,000
Plus a sign-on bonus.

Universities Microsoft plans to visit in 2007-8
Aston, Bath, Birmingham, Brunel, Cambridge, Glasgow, Kent, Leeds, Loughborough, Manchester, Oxford Brookes, Reading, Warwick
Please check with your university careers service for details of events.

Application deadline
January 2008

Contact Details
✉ gradrec@microsoft.com
Turn to page 224 now to request more information about Microsoft.

Microsoft have created an environment where people can do their best. Hard work is expected, but their graduates and students are free to satisfy their intellectual curiosity. Microsoft is somewhere people can think along new lines, explore truly exciting technologies and actually enjoy spending time.

The people who flourish at Microsoft are natural communicators with inquisitive natures, a passion for technology and an instinctive understanding of customers. But what really sets them apart is a drive that raises them above the average whether they join commercial or technical business groups.

The 'Microsoft Academy for University Hires' provides the perfect transition between academic and professional life. Although challenging, it equips graduates with the professional skills and know-how required for a rewarding and successful career at Microsoft. Graduates will tackle unchartered territory, whether working in a technical, sales or marketing role. It might mean discovering how others work or thinking along new lines. Either way, successful applicants will be stepping outside their comfort zone.

The graduate programme includes residential courses at international locations and self-directed learning. Graduates will be given real responsibility, whilst also having the support of managers and mentors throughout. The basic requirements are a 2:1, creativity, vision, people skills, an inquiring mind and a willingness to learn.

The emphasis during student placements in Reading or London is on supplementing theory learnt at university with real, practical experience. The 48-week scheme starts in July with a week-long induction. Training can include residential courses and self-directed learning.

Stunned

Eager

Absorbed

Career

Whatever you do at Microsoft, express yourself.

The Microsoft Academy for University Hires (MACH) is a two year programme designed to take passionate graduates and set them on one of many diverse careers paths across our technical, sales and marketing groups.

Over the course of the programme, we'll provide you with the theoretical and practical skills you need to complement your academic achievements. We'll also ensure that you have the business acumen to make a real difference at the highest levels. By the time you graduate from MACH, you'll have the language to express yourself compellingly, the tools to take on any challenge and the ability to deliver solutions with the power to touch the lives of people all over the world.

Graduate to a more expressive future:

www.microsoft.com/uk/graduates

Microsoft®
Your potential. Our passion.™

Morgan Stanley

www.morganstanley.com/careers/recruiting

Vacancies for around 250 graduates in 2008

- Finance
- Investment Banking
- IT

Vacancies also available in Europe, Asia, the USA and elsewhere in the world.

Starting salary for 2008
£Competitive

Universities that Morgan Stanley plans to visit in 2007-8
Aston, Bath, Birmingham, Bristol, Cambridge, City, Dublin, Durham, Edinburgh, Glasgow, Kent, London, Manchester, Nottingham, Oxford, Sheffield, Southampton, St Andrews, Strathclyde, Warwick, York
Please check with your university careers service for details of events.

Application deadline
11th November 2007

Contact Details
✉ campusrecruiting-europe@morganstanley.com
☎ 0207 425 8000 ext. 4257575

Turn to page 224 now to request more information about Morgan Stanley.

Morgan Stanley is one of the largest and most respected financial services companies, with a longstanding reputation for excellence on a global scale.

Morgan Stanley's 45,000 employees in 31 countries work as one firm across geographic and product boundaries. Their services to institutions, governments and individuals include: investment banking advice on mergers and acquisitions, privatisations and financial restructuring; underwriting debt and equity; sales and trading in all the world's major markets; and insightful research. They also manage more than $560 billion of investments, from traditional mutual funds to 'alternative' investments such as real estate and private equity, and specialise in serving affluent individuals around the world.

Analyst training at Morgan Stanley quickly makes effective professionals. Through a structured programme, graduates receive an intensive induction on how to use Morgan Stanley's unsurpassed data resources and analytic tools.

Graduates work on a team under the direct guidance of senior professionals who are among the best in their fields. They will give as much responsibility as graduates can handle, in an environment that affords exciting opportunities to work with a wide variety of clients in different industries, helping them to make strategic decisions involving capital raising, research or trading issues at the highest level. Training is not limited to the first weeks or months on the job but is ongoing throughout a career at Morgan Stanley.

Morgan Stanley accepts applications from all degree types. They are looking for candidates with a keen intellect, excellent communication skills, analytical aptitude and high dedication to their professional responsibilities.

Connect with opportunities worldwide

Morgan Stanley could be you. It's people who make Morgan Stanley stand out. Come discover a diverse group who share one mission: to create the world's finest financial thinking, products and services. Learn about the rich variety of opportunities we offer.

At Morgan Stanley you can work with people who are the best in the business— and enjoy what they do.

VISIT AND APPLY ONLINE AT WWW.MORGANSTANLEY.COM/CAREERS/RECRUITING

NATIONAL GRADUATE
DEVELOPMENT PROGRAMME

ngdp.

FOR LOCAL GOVERNMENT

www.ngdp.co.uk

Vacancies for around
70+ graduates in 2008

■ General Management

Starting salary for 2008
£21,588
With London weighting.
National salary rise pending.

Universities that ngdp
plans to visit in 2007-8
Please check with your university
careers service for details of events.

Application deadline
14th January 2008

Contact Details
✉ enquiries@ngdp.co.uk
☎ 0845 222 0250
Turn to page 224 now to request
more information about ngdp.

The ngdp is a two-year graduate development programme,
run by the Improvement and Development Agency (The IDeA)
that is designed to develop future managers and leaders in
local government.

It was set up to provide local government with the high calibre managers their
communities need, and to give committed graduates the training, qualifications
and opportunities to make a real difference. Local government is the largest
employer in the UK, with over two million staff in over 400 local authorities and
in excess of 500 different occupational areas.

Over 250 graduates have completed the programme and many now hold
important managerial and policy roles in the sector. Local government is
going through many positive changes at present and as a trainee on the
ngdp, graduates will be at the forefront of these changes.

The programme consists of placements in key areas of local authority service
and offer a range of experiences designed to provide a broad understanding
of many aspects of local government, including: strategy, service delivery
and support service.

Trainees will participate in the IDeA Graduate Leadership Academy, which
combines study for a bespoke Postgraduate Diploma in Local Government
Management at Warwick Business School with soft skill development training.
Mentoring also provided on a regional basis and programme support is
provided through a dedicated central ngdp team.

Other graduate entry routes into local government can be found at
www.LGtalent.com

work, work, work, work, work, work, work, work, work, work,
work, work, work, work, work, work, work, work, work, work,
work, work, work, work, work, work, work, work, work, work,
work, work, work, work, work, work, work, work, work, work,
work, work, work, work, work, work, work, work, work, work,
work, work, work, work, work, work, work, work, work, work,
work, work, work, work, work, work, work, work, work, work,
work, work, work, work, work, work, work, work, work, work,
work, work, work, work, work, work, work, work, work, work,
work, work, work, work, work, work, work, work, work, life...

Vacancies for around 220 graduates in 2008

- Finance
- General Management
- Human Resources

Starting salary for 2008
£Competitive

Universities that the NHS plans to visit in 2007-8

Aston, Bath, Birmingham, Bristol, Cambridge, Durham, East Anglia, Exeter, Lancaster, Leeds, Liverpool, London, Manchester, Newcastle, Nottingham, Oxford, Reading, Sheffield, Southampton, Warwick, York
Please check with your university careers service for details of events.

Application deadline
30th November 2007
For intake in September 2008.

Contact Details
✉ nhsgraduates@tmpw.co.uk

Turn to page 224 now to request more information about the NHS.

The NHS offer three dedicated streams into graduate management – finance, HR and general management training. All have one aim: to develop managers and leaders of the future who will be required for providing a world class, patient-led health and health care system.

In 2000 the number of outpatients waiting more than three months was 393,000. Today, that figure is just 126 people. The number of people waiting longer than six months for treatment as an inpatient fell from 269,000 in 2000 to just 126 today. This ongoing transformation means that there has never been a better time for ambitious, talented graduates to join them.

The NHS Graduate Management scheme is a 2-year programme and has a combination of core learning and specialised threads that support the attainment of a professional qualification in either human resources, finance or general management. Specialist training is at the heart of the scheme, supporting development of personal qualities and management skills. Trainees from each specialism learn together, building relationships across management functions for the future and are supported through their own senior mentor. Personal development continues in years 3 and 4, ensuring trainees are part of the NHS talent pool. A number of their ex trainees have reached Chief Executive level within the Department of Health.

The NHS actively encourage applicants from all backgrounds who have or are expecting a 2:2 degree. Postgraduates, mature students and those working within the NHS are encouraged to apply. Other qualifications may be accepted – please see the website for eligibility criteria.

You could go to work
for the 99 other companies,

or you could come to life

Some careers are just about work. In the NHS, it's rather more important than that. The chances are that we're the very first organisation you ever used. For many, we'll also be the last. In between, we're here to help all of us, in sickness and in health. As you're reading this we're changing lives, keeping families together, giving people hope. In the past 7 days we have helped 1.4 million people at home, delivered 10,000 babies, treated 150,000 pairs of feet and mended 3,000 broken hearts. Other employers offer you attractive benefits packages, excellent starting salaries and exceptional training and development. We do too. But we also give you something that is totally unique at work. And that's life. Apply online at www.bringingleadershiptolife.nhs.uk

npower

Vacancies for around 60 graduates in 2008

- Engineering
- Finance
- General Management
- Human Resources
- IT

Starting salary for 2008
£23,000+

Universities that npower plans to visit in 2007-8
Please check with your university careers service for details of events.

Application deadline
See website for full details.

Contact Details
✉ enquiry@gradweb.co.uk

Turn to page 224 now to request more information about npower.

As Britain's brightest energy company with over 10,000 employees across the UK, npower gives creative and ambitious graduates the chance to work on exciting projects, such as the renewable energy contract powering Wembley Stadium's illuminated arch. They are one of the UK's leading integrated energy companies, and part of RWE, one of Europe's largest utility groups.

They operate one of the largest portfolios of power generating plants in the UK and supply electricity and gas to more than 6.8 million residential and business customers. Leaders in the UK renewable energy market, they are constantly developing innovative energy-related technologies. npower take their role in the community very seriously and for the last three years have been in the Business in the Community (BitC) Corporate Response Index top twenty.

At npower, graduates can join schemes across the whole of the business – engineering, commercial and risk, finance, HR, on the IS scheme within their Systems division and as business generalists. Graduates swiftly become important members of their chosen team, gain insights into different areas of the business and are given responsibility at an early stage. Each scheme has an excellent training programme and all graduates are given mentors right from the start.

The quality of its people is just one of the reasons why npower is Britain's brightest energy company – npower offers challenging career opportunities in a creative and exciting culture. To find out more about npower and their graduate opportunities, please go to www.brightergraduates.com

Who said that clean energy was just an electric dream? At npower we've created 'Juice' energy which comes from renewable resources such as our very own wind farms. These wind farms produce enough power to boil nearly a billion kettles a year (give or take the odd peppermint tea), and we don't charge our customers anything to switch over to using it.

Because with us, it's not just about making sure the nation can enjoy a nice cup of coffee. We need to think about the environment and answer the questions that are fuelling the UK energy agenda right now. Which is why we need some seriously bright graduates to work on these issues from day one. So whether you join us in engineering, commercial and risk, HR, finance, as a business generalist, or on our IS scheme within our Systems division, we'll make sure the one question you're not asking is "do you take sugar with that?"

Find out more about the energy company that won't go off the boil by visiting www.brightergraduates.com

Who squeezes every drop of goodness out of their juice?

npower

RWE Group

Oxfam

www.oxfam.org.uk/interns

**Vacancies for around
100 graduates in 2008**

- Accountancy
- Finance
- General Management
- Human Resources
- IT
- Logistics
- Marketing
- Media
- Research & Development
- Retailing

Starting salary for 2008
£Voluntary

**Universities that Oxfam
plans to visit in 2007-8**
Please check with your university
careers service for details of events.

Application deadline
Year-round recruitment

Contact Details
✉ internship@oxfam.org.uk

Turn to page 224 now to request
more information about Oxfam.

**Oxfam GB is a development, relief, and campaigning
organisation, which is working towards a world without poverty.**

Oxfam is about people. People are its greatest resource: over 22,000
volunteers help run Oxfam's famous shops; over 600,000 individuals
make regular donations; more than a million people worldwide support its
campaigns; and countless individuals work in more than 80 countries, with
Oxfam, to find lasting solutions to overcome poverty and suffering.

Oxfam is looking for committed, enthusiastic and professional people to
take part in its voluntary Internship Scheme. For those who are passionate
about the work and high values of Oxfam, and are willing to take on
responsibility in this high-profile charity, this could be an ideal opportunity.
Interns may expect to work on specific projects, carry out research,
develop campaigns, trial new ideas, help manage an Oxfam shop, plan
and facilitate an Oxfam event, and more, depending on the internship
they apply for.

The Oxfam Internship Scheme is divided into three intakes throughout the year;
January to May, June to August and September to December. Although it is
unpaid, the scheme will reimburse reasonable local travel and lunch expenses.
Flexible hours also allow participants to have a part-time job. Oxfam's
Internships are based throughout out the UK, in some of our 750 shops,
our 8 regional offices and in our Head Office in Oxford.

If graduates have what it takes to inspire others to change the world there is
no better place to do it than Oxfam! For more information and to view current
vacancies please go to the website.

Some companies will offer you the world.

We'll give you the chance to change it.

Voluntary Internship Opportunities | UK-wide

Join Oxfam and you can expect real responsibility.
Wherever you join us, you'll be able to look back and
say you've helped to make the world a better place.

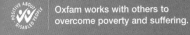

Oxfam works with others to
overcome poverty and suffering.   Reg Charity No. 202918

Possible vacancies in 2008

- Accountancy
- Finance
- Human Resources
- Law
- Marketing
- Media
- Purchasing
- Sales

Starting salary for 2008
£18,720
Plus benefits.

Universities that Penguin plans to visit in 2007-8
Please check with your university careers service for details of events.

Application deadline
Year-round recruitment

Contact Details
Turn to page 224 now to request more information about Penguin.

Words are just the beginning of Penguin Books' business, and for their people they're about so much more than what is seen on the page. Perhaps it's because for more than seventy years now they've been the publisher everyone looks to not just for great books, but also for innovation and for how to act with dignity and integrity.

They're always looking for different points of view, new voices and ways of working – and they're always happy to listen to new ideas. Which is why they have publishing's first green committee and diversity panel; why they have the leading publisher blog, podcast and website; and why last year they won all the major UK literary prizes as well as the Sales and Marketing 'Nibbie' for the second successive year – and ultimately why they were crowned Publisher of the Year at the 2007 British Book Awards.

They have opportunities for accountants, designers, publicists, marketers, production controllers, sales, rights and operations people – oh and for editorial and publishing staff, too. And with the Penguin family including Dorling Kindersley, Rough Guides, Puffin, Ladybird and Fredrick Warne, located in offices from London to the US, Australia, India and New Zealand, they're always looking for people prepared to think big.

No one is doing more to move publishing forward in the twenty-first century than Penguin. Facing the challenges of the digital revolution and ensuring that books of all shapes and sizes remain the cornerstone of a thriving culture will take some smart thinking and some innovative solutions – and not a few good words.

REASONS TO BECOME A PENGUIN

1) You get to work closely with your favourite authors. Now what could be more fun than that? **2) We're a diverse bunch.** And we think publishing should be for everyone. **3) We're the greenest publishers in town.** We work with the Woodland Trust and our books are printed on FSC accredited paper. **4) Our award-winning publishing.** In 2006 we won the Man Booker, Orange and Whitbread prizes. **5) We know how to celebrate.** Our birthday parties and anniversary publishing have become the stuff of legend. **6) To prove publishing isn't stuffy we play at the cutting edge of the digital revolution.** Look us up at www.penguin.co.uk, find us in Second Life and come and have a chat with us on our blog. **7) People pay attention to what we do.** They just do. They can't help it. **8) We're the only publishing company in here.** Go on, check, but don't forget to come back here and finish the list. **9) You never need to explain what your company does at parties.** When you say 'I work for Penguin', everyone gets just a little bit jealous. **10) Your mum and dad will love you forever ...** (at least that's what our mums and dads tell us).

PUBLISHER
OF THE YEAR
2 0 0 7

CELEBRATE WITH US AT:
www.penguincelebrations.com

read more
www.penguin.co.uk

COULD YOU?
POLICE

www.policecouldyou.co.uk and www.policehighpotential.org.uk

Vacancies for unlimited graduates in 2008

■ All sectors

Starting salary for 2008
£21,000

Universities that HPD plans to visit in 2007-8
Please check with your university careers service for details of events.

Application deadline
Year-round recruitment

Contact Details
☎ 020 7021 7070
Turn to page 224 now to request more information about HPD.

A career in the police offers an exciting mix of challenge and reward. Policing in today's modern service involves reducing crime and the fear of crime, working in partnership with the public, supporting victims and witnesses whilst using the latest technology to assist with the detection and prevention of crime.

The challenges faced by police officers are often mental rather than physical, requiring an understanding of what makes people behave as they do, and to use that knowledge to form strong policing skills.

The modern police force offers careers with many opportunities to enter specialist roles; traffic, fraud, Criminal Investigation Department (CID), Special Branch (combating terrorism and other serious crime), dog handlers and mounted officers, are just a few. There are also great prospects to move up the career ladder into senior leadership positions.

Graduates from any discipline who have secured employment as a police officer with one of the forces in England, Northern Ireland or Wales may then be eligible to join the Police High Potential Development Scheme (HPDS). HPDS provides development opportunities and structured support aimed at broadening members' experience of the police service, and preparing them for strategic leadership roles.

Joining the police offers a starting salary of around £21,000 p.a. upon commencing service, rising to around £23,500 p.a. on completion of the initial training (salaries for Metropolitan Police and City of London Police attract a London Weighting supplement).

The HPD scheme is funded by the National Policing Improvement Agency (NPIA). Go to www.npia.police.uk for more information about the NPIA.

I'VE BUILT UP 16 COMPANIES, BUT I COULDN'T REBUILD THE MORALE OF A TEAM OF OFFICERS WORKING ON A CHILD ABUSE CASE.

Stelios Haji-Ioannou
Founder of easyGroup

If you think you could, apply to join the Police and ask about the **High Potential Development Scheme. Call 020 7021 7070 or** visit our website at policehighpotential.org.uk to find out more.

COULD YOU?

POLICE

PRICEWATERHOUSE COOPERS 🏦

Vacancies for around 1,200 graduates in 2008

- Accountancy
- Consulting
- Finance
- Law

Starting salary for 2008
£Competitive
Plus flexible benefits and an interest-free loan.

Universities that PricewaterhouseCoopers plans to visit in 2007-8
Please check with your university careers service for details of events.

Application deadline
Varies by Function
See website for full details.

Contact Details
☎ 0800 100 2200 or
+44 (0)121 265 5852

Turn to page 224 now to request more information about PricewaterhouseCoopers.

PricewaterhouseCoopers LLP (PwC) is the one firm for all talented graduates. As one of the world's largest professional services firms they have a lot to offer. Exciting opportunities, with an enviable range of clients – from public and private companies to governments and charities – they work in partnership with clients to create leading-edge solutions.

Whether the degree is art or science related, PricewaterhouseCoopers offer breadth of career opportunity where graduates can build on the skills and experience they've gained at university, and tailor and develop their career. They expect a 2:1 and at least a 280 UCAS tariff or equivalent. But just as important are the personal qualities, enthusiasm and ideas graduates bring.

PwC offer a wide range of possibilities within their business groups, each of which boasts an eye-catching client list. Some of their groups are renowned as breeding grounds for the best business minds in their field. Others are at the forefront of developments in the challenging e-business arena.

Wherever successful applicants join they'll need to be prepared to work hard from day one and in return they will benefit from the development experience PwC invest in their people together with the breadth that the variety of work they can offer. In return for talent and commitment, they pay a competitive salary and have an innovative flexible benefits scheme.

To find out more about the opportunities on offer and to apply online, please visit – www.pwc.com/uk/careers/

**Nationwide Opportunities
Spring and Autumn 2008**

Assurance
Tax
Advisory
Actuarial
Strategy

There really is only one option. If you want more variety in terms of the work you do, the projects you work on and the clients you work with, the sheer scope of our activities makes us the obvious choice. Right from the start you'll have alternatives. Our structured development plan gives you the chance to specialise within a specific business area. Or you can decide to experience a number of different areas, picking up valuable technical, business and personal skills as you go. Just bring us a 2:1 in any subject, at least a 280 UCAS tariff or equivalent, and plenty of enthusiasm and ideas, and see where they can take you. We're the one firm for all choosy graduates.

www.pwc.com/uk/careers/

Text: PwC to 85792

We value diversity in our people.

P&G

**Vacancies for around
150 graduates in 2008**

- Accountancy
- Engineering
- Finance
- General Management
- Human Resources
- IT
- Logistics
- Manufacturing
- Marketing
- Purchasing
- Research & Development
- Sales

Vacancies also available in Europe.

Starting salary for 2008
£27,040

**Universities that
Procter & Gamble
plans to visit in 2007-8**
Birmingham, Cambridge,
Dublin, Durham, Edinburgh,
Leeds, London, Manchester,
Nottingham, Oxford,
Strathclyde, Warwick
Please check with your university
careers service for details of events.

Application deadline
Year-round recruitment

Contact Details
✉ recunitedkingdm.im@pg.com

Turn to page 224 now to request more
information about Procter & Gamble.

Established 170 years ago, P&G is, according to Fortune
Magazine, the most admired household and personal goods
company in the world. It has one of the largest portfolios of
trusted, quality brands, including Ariel, Always, Bounty, Braun,
Charmin, Crest, Duracell, Gillette, Head & Shoulders, Iams,
Lenor, Olay, OralB, Pampers, Pantene and Pringles.

Every day these brands touch the lives of more than three billion people
around the world. 140,000 P&G people in 80 countries worldwide work to
ensure P&G brands live up to their promise to make everyday life a little better.

P&G attracts and recruits the finest people in the world, because it grows and
develops its senior managers from within the organisation. This means new
starters with P&G can expect a job with responsibility from day one and a
career with a variety of challenging roles that develop and broaden their skills,
together with the support of training and coaching to help them succeed.

P&G offers exciting careers in all the functions required to operate a major
multinational company. These include customer business development (sales
& commercial careers), finance, human resources, information decisions &
solutions (careers adding value to business processes through IT), marketing
(careers in brand management), product supply (careers in engineering,
purchasing, manufacturing and supply chain management) and research
and development. The company looks for talented graduates with a broad
range of skills demonstrated through activities and interests. Most functions
welcome applicants from any degree discipline, product supply requires an
engineering degree and R&D requires an engineering or science degree.

challenge

Are you ready to face a new challenge every day?

A career with Procter & Gamble offers roles with real responsibility from day one with the training and coaching to help you succeed. With $22 billion brands and operations across 80 countries, you will find your work really does bring a new challenge every day!

Add to this P&G's approach to growing our top leadership within the organisation and you will understand why your continuing development is so important to our success.

If you are ready for this challenge then we are ready for you! Apply online at **www.pgcareers.com** for vacancies throughout Europe.

- CBD/Sales
- Product Supply
- Finance & Accounting
- Information and Decision Solutions

- Marketing
- Research & Development
- Human Resources

To find out more visit 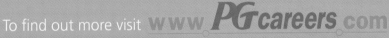 www.**PG**careers.com

P&G a new challenge every day

REUTERS

www.reuters.com/careers/graduate

**Vacancies for around
40 graduates in 2008**

- Accountancy
- Finance
- IT
- Media

Starting salary for 2008
£26,000-£27,500

**Universities that Reuters
plans to visit in 2007-8**
Please check with your university
careers service for details of events.

Application deadline
31st December 2007

Contact Details
✉ graduate.recruitment@
reuters.com
Turn to page 224 now to request
more information about Reuters.

WHAT YOU DO HERE

Reuters is a dynamic business, delivering financial data and international news to a global audience of more than a billion people daily. In trading rooms, newsrooms and living rooms the world over, the Reuters name is a watchword for fast, accurate and unbiased information.

It's a fascinating, challenging, fast-moving environment to work in – one that gives graduates a chance to make a real and immediate difference to the world around them.

There are four routes into Reuters for graduates. The Business programme is split into a number of placements within Reuters' functions and is designed to give graduates first-hand experience of how the company operates. On the Finance programme successful applicants get the best of both worlds – studying for the CIMA professional qualification while also gaining hands-on experience throughout the business. Technology drives everything Reuters does, so the Technology programme will put graduates right at the heart of the company where they'll work with truly world-class systems and products. The Reuters Journalism programme is one of the most sought-after training opportunities in the profession and will give graduates a chance to learn from the best in the business.

Whatever the programme, successful applicants will find themselves doing real work right from the start, exploring this incredibly diverse business and probably spending some time overseas. Longer term, they'll be encouraged to shape their own career development – and this is a company where they will never be short of options.

WILL BE FELT EVERYWHERE

Be influential from day one – join an organisation
that shapes decision-making around the world.

REUTERS

Rolls-Royce

www.rolls-royce.com/university

Vacancies for around 160 graduates in 2008

- Engineering
- Finance
- Human Resources
- Logistics
- Manufacturing
- Purchasing

Starting salary for 2008
£24,500-£27,000

Universities Rolls-Royce plans to visit in 2007-8
Aston, Bath, Birmingham, Bristol, Cambridge, Cardiff, Durham, Loughborough, Manchester, Nottingham, Oxford, Sheffield, Southampton, Strathclyde, Warwick
Please check with your university careers service for details of events.

Application deadline
Year-round recruitment

Contact Details
✉ peoplelink@rolls-royce.com

Turn to page 224 now to request more information about Rolls-Royce.

Graduates know Rolls-Royce as a high technology engineering company that's a global market leader in power generation on land, sea and in the air. But there's even more to Rolls-Royce than people think.

With civil aerospace, defence aerospace, marine and energy businesses, Rolls-Royce develops innovative solutions to address today's burning issues. Issues such as how to meet the world's demand for air travel, while reducing its effect on the environment. And, with 37,000 employees based on five continents, they're working on some of the most exciting projects around – including developing the world's lowest emission engines for the new Airbus A380 and creating technology that could change ship propulsion forever.

In a highly competitive global market-place, Rolls-Royce need the most efficient supply chain, the most switched-on finance operation, the most creative deal-makers, the best-organised project managers, the greatest customer focus and the finest engineers to continue to succeed. There are two main programmes specifically for graduates. The Professional Excellence Programme lasts 12-18 months and offers the chance to develop a high level of competence in a particular career area. The Leadership Development Programme lasts for 18-24 months and focuses on developing leadership skills in a particular business function.

These programmes are tailored to meet the individual needs of the graduate. Working closely with an Early Career Development Advisor, graduates can design an approach that combines practical experience, formal training, project work and other activities to enable them to perform to their potential.

"Today I opened up the world for someone."
What will you do tomorrow?

Engineering · Finance · Supply Chain · Operations Management · HR · Commercial · Customer Management · Marketing · Project Management

Graduate opportunities

Our graduates are proud to work for us. No wonder, when they're involved in exciting, innovative projects such as engineering the world's lowest emission aircraft engines and working in partnership with major suppliers and customers.

We've been an icon of innovative thinking and excellence for over a century in the civil and defence aerospace, energy and marine sectors. We offer a wealth of opportunities through two graduate programmes designed specifically to develop your professional or leadership skills to the full. So, what will you do tomorrow? To find out more, just visit www.rolls-royce.com/university

Trusted to deliver excellence

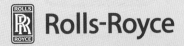 Rolls-Royce

The Royal Bank of Scotland Group

Vacancies for around 550 graduates in 2008

- Accountancy
- Finance
- Human Resources
- Investment Banking
- IT
- Marketing
- Retailing
- Sales

Vacancies also available in Europe, Asia, the USA and elsewhere in the world.

Starting salary for 2008
£Competitive

Universities that the Royal Bank of Scotland Group plans to visit in 2007-8

Aston, Bath, Belfast, Bristol, Dublin, Edinburgh, Exeter, Glasgow, Leeds, Liverpool, London, Loughborough, Manchester, Newcastle, Nottingham, Sheffield, St Andrews, Strathclyde, York
Please check with your university careers service for details of events.

Application deadline
Varies by function
See website for full details.

Contact Details

✉ rbsgrads@tmpw.co.uk

Turn to page 224 now to request more information about The Royal Bank of Scotland Group.

The Royal Bank of Scotland Group doesn't stand still. They entered US banking with the acquisition of Citizens Bank and are now a top-ten US commercial banking business. They completed the biggest takeover in British banking history and now have the largest retail network in the UK.

The RBS group's partnership with the Bank of China has positioned them as a major player in the world's fastest growing economy.

With brands including NatWest, Churchill, Direct Line and Coutts, they are making it happen for more than 30 million customers and 137,000 staff worldwide.

RBS has over 550 graduate opportunities, ranging from Group Technology and Risk to Retail and Finance, and from Coutts to HR. They also run a number of placements, to give students a real taste of life at one of the world's largest financial services groups.

As one might expect from a group their size, graduates will be supported via a network of buddies and mentors as well as formal and on-the-job training. They will also have the opportunity to continue studying for professional qualifications or take part in many of their group-funded community programmes to develop skills such as leadership, communication and team working.

Graduates will need at least a 2:1 in any discipline – combined with the focus and tenacity to deliver in a truly international organisation. In return, they can be sure of real responsibility and continued development from day one.

keep main path

It means nothing until you **make it happen**

Worked it out yet? Good. Because if you want to get ahead here at The Royal Bank of Scotland Group, you need to be able to think for yourself, take on new challenges and get things done. We offer over 15 graduate programmes in everything from Group Technology and Risk to Retail and Finance, and from Coutts to HR. And whichever one you choose, there's plenty of scope for you to make things happen. Find out more at **www.makeitrbs.com**

Make it happen

RBS
The Royal Bank of Scotland Group

Sainsbury's

www.sainsburys.co.uk/graduates

**Vacancies for around
110 graduates in 2008**

- Finance
- Human Resources
- IT
- Logistics
- Marketing
- Purchasing
- Retailing

**Starting salary for 2008
£Competitive**

**Universities Sainsbury's
plans to visit in 2007-8**

Aston, Bath, Birmingham,
Bristol, Cardiff, Durham,
East Anglia, Essex, Exeter,
Glasgow, Heriot-Watt,
Lancaster, Leeds,
London, Loughborough,
Manchester, Newcastle,
Northumbria, Nottingham,
Nottingham Trent, Reading,
Sheffield, Southampton,
Surrey, Sussex,
Warwick, York
Please check with your university
careers service for details of events.

Application deadline
See website for full details.

Contact Details

☎ 020 7695 6000

Turn to page 224 now to request
more information about Sainsbury's.

Sainsbury's is a leading FTSE 100 company and a very
high-profile name in a fast-moving market. The success of
the brand re-launch, and the suggestion to customers that
they 'try something new today' has been a resounding
success in re-establishing Sainsbury's in the hearts and
minds of their customers.

Sainsbury's need bright, savvy graduates, who, regardless of their particular
field of interest, love the buzz of retail and are hungry for success. Their
schemes offer exceptional graduates the opportunity to develop leadership
qualities, to gain practical business skills, and to increase their capabilities
through formal and informal training, all within the context of a fast-paced
retail organisation.

Graduates can choose from 10 schemes, each with its own structure and – in
some cases – professional qualification. The roles are in buying, customer
& marketing, finance, HR, IT, product development and technology, supply
chain, commercial, property, retail and summer placements.

An essential element of every scheme is a three to six-month in-store
placement. Sainsbury's believe that without the grounding and context that
exposure to the hectic realities of a busy retail environment provides, expertise
in any area, from HR to IT, isn't gained without understanding its impact on the
people at the very heart of their business; their customers.

But first things first: find out more about what makes a business like theirs
tick at www.sainsburys.co.uk/graduates, and find out what it takes to have the
drive and passion to join forces with Sainsbury's.

BRIGHT · SAVVY
FAIR · LIVELY
BRAVE · CURIOUS

HUNGRY

Not everyone will share our determination and hunger for success, but if you do, and you want to work with a leading business that will satisfy your hunger with commitments and action, you should think seriously about joining forces with us.

OPEN · FRESH
KEEN · CREATIVE
RESILIENT · TRUE

If you are hungry for success
and want to find out more visit
www.sainsburys.co.uk/graduates

Sainsbury's
Try something new today

www.shell.com/careers

Vacancies for around 300 graduates in 2008

- Engineering
- Finance
- Human Resources
- IT
- Marketing
- Research & Development
- Sales

Starting salary for 2008
£29,500
Including benefits.

Universities that Shell plans to visit in 2007-8
Aberdeen, Bath, Birmingham, Bristol, Cambridge, Dublin, Durham, Edinburgh, Heriot-Watt, Leeds, London, Loughborough, Manchester, Nottingham, Oxford, Sheffield, Southampton, Strathclyde, Warwick
Please check with your university careers service for details of events.

Application deadline
Year-round recruitment

Contact Details
✉ graduates@shell.com
☎ 0845 600 1819

Turn to page 224 now to request more information about Shell.

Pursue it
A more exciting
career experience

Achieving more together

Shell is at the heart of the energy and petrochemical business and is one of the world's most successful organisations. They are totally committed to a business strategy that always balances profits with principles. They are also committed to attracting, training, developing and rewarding world class people for this truly world class business.

From the moment graduates join Shell, their development is of prime importance. Learning by doing, supported by their manager, is key – real responsibility and decision-making are part of life at Shell from day one. Career progression depends entirely on individual ability, talent and ambition.

Working for Shell, graduates could potentially move geographically, functionally and between different businesses. Shell have a strong ethic of promotion from within, supported by a global job opportunity intranet site.

Graduates' academic records are one key factor in assessing applications, but Shell also place emphasis on performance during interviews and assessment centres. Shell have identified capacity, achievement and relationships as critical to high performance.

Shell have a number of pre-employment opportunities: the Shell Gourami Business Challenge, for which applications are welcome from students who will be in their final year when Gourami takes place; the Personal Development Award, for which applications are welcome from non-finalists.

Full details on Shell can be found on their website, www.shell.com/careers

CONTRACTING & PROCUREMENT
FINANCE
HUMAN RESOURCES
INFORMATION TECHNOLOGY
SALES & MARKETING
SUPPLY & DISTRIBUTION
TRADING
GEOLOGY/GEOPHYSICS
PETROPHYSICS
PRODUCTION TECHNOLOGY
PRODUCT/PROCESS RESEARCH
ENGINEERING:
RESERVOIR/PETROLEUM
WELL
PRODUCTION
PROCESS
ASSET MAINTENANCE
PROJECT/FACILITIES
DISCIPLINE

With the wind behind you and open space ahead, there's no limit to the possible directions your career could take. And at Shell, we'll support you all the way.

Our approach is collaborative – matching our business needs with your training needs, our global opportunities with your career aspirations. We aim to build a win-win partnership between you and Shell.

Right from the start, you'll be making a valuable contribution to exciting projects. Your ideas will be taken on board, your talent recognised and achievements rewarded.

So if you want to achieve more in your career, get together with Shell. You can make your online application right now – just visit our career website.

Shell is an Equal Opportunity Employer
www.shell.com/careers

Explore it
There's a wider world out there

Achieving more together

SLAUGHTER AND MAY

Vacancies for around 85-95 graduates in 2008
For training contracts starting in 2010

 Law

Starting salary for 2008
£36,000

Universities that Slaughter and May plans to visit in 2007-8
Please check with your university careers service for details of events.

Application deadline
Year-round recruitment

Contact Details
✉ trainee.recruit@
slaughterandmay.com

Turn to page 224 now to request more information about Slaughter and May.

Slaughter and May is a leading international law firm whose principal areas of practice are in the fields of corporate, commercial and financing law.

The firm's clients range from the world's leading multinationals to venture capital start-ups. They include public and private companies, governments and non-governmental organisations, commercial and investment banks. The lawyers devise solutions for complex, often transnational, problems and advise some of the world's brightest business minds.

Their overseas offices and close working relationships with leading independent law firms in other jurisdictions mean there are opportunities to work in places such as Auckland, Brussels, Berlin, Copenhagen, Düsseldorf, Frankfurt, Helsinki, Hong Kong, Luxembourg, Madrid, Milan, New York, Oslo, Paris, Prague, Rome, Singapore, Stockholm and Tokyo.

Approximately 85-95 training contracts are available per year for trainee solicitors. Slaughter and May also offers two-week work experience schemes at Christmas, Easter and during the summer for those considering a career in law.

Following Law School, there is a two year training period during which time trainee solicitors gain experience of a broad cross-section of the firm's practice by taking an active part in the work of four or five groups, sharing an office with a partner or experienced associate. In addition, Slaughter and May offers an extensive training programme of lectures, seminars and courses with discussion groups covering general and specialised legal topics.

Applications from candidates of good 2.1 ability from any discipline are considered. Please visit the website for further information.

Forget the clichés about training with a major law firm. It's not about what you know, who you know or where you went to university. It's about what you can learn. And if you have a good degree (not necessarily in law), an inquiring mind and an ability to meet challenges, training at Slaughter and May could be the best possible route to a worthwhile, stimulating and rewarding career.

Great minds think differently.

SLAUGHTER AND MAY

LEARN MORE about training contracts and work experience schemes at one of the world's most respected law firms by contacting:

Charlotte Houghton, Slaughter and May, One Bunhill Row, London EC1Y 8YY. Telephone 020 7600 1200.

www.slaughterandmay.com

Teach First
LEARNING TO LEAD

Vacancies for around 360 graduates in 2008

■ All Sectors

Starting salary for 2008
£Competitive

Universities Teach First plans to visit in 2007-8
Please check with your university careers service for details of events.

Application deadline
Final: 28th March 2008
See website for full details.

Contact Details
✉ faq@teachfirst.org.uk

Turn to page 224 now to request more information about Teach First.

Teach First is a unique two-year opportunity for graduates to be different and to achieve something special. Energy, intelligence and creativity can transform the futures of students in challenging schools around the UK. At the same time it's an opportunity to dramatically enhance individual career potential and to make a tangible difference to society.

Teach First takes exceptional graduates and transforms them into inspiring leaders – their leadership, inspiration and above all their example can be the key that unlocks the future of students confronted by a wide range of personal and social issues.

And while graduates are transforming the lives of young people in schools around the country, Teach First will help them to maximise their own potential. With high-quality training – leading to the achievement of Qualified Teacher Status – leadership development and supportive coaching and alumni programmes, Teach First will provide successful applicants with a strong platform of skills and experience to take forward into any future management career. That's why over 80 companies, government agencies and public bodies back Teach First to develop top talent for the future.

There is no question that Teach First is an extremely demanding option. After just six weeks graduates will be delivering real lessons to real students. But if Teach First is uniquely challenging, it is also uniquely satisfying. Few other options offer the same degree of genuine responsibility so early. And rarely, if ever, will graduates have the opportunity to make such a direct and important difference.

TESCO

www.tesco-graduates.com

Vacancies for around 250+ graduates in 2008

- Accountancy
- Consulting
- Engineering
- Finance
- Human Resources
- IT
- Law
- Logistics
- Marketing
- Media
- Purchasing
- Research & Development
- Retailing

Starting salary for 2008
£Competitive

Universities that Tesco plans to visit in 2007-8
Bristol, Cambridge, London, Loughborough, Manchester, Oxford, Reading, Southampton, Warwick
Please check with your university careers service for details of events.

Application deadline
December 2007

Contact Details
✉ graduate.recruitment@uk.tesco.com

Turn to page 224 now to request more information about Tesco.

Tesco offers a variety of graduate career development opportunities. Not to mention providing everything from iPods to clothing, and sofas to stirrups. Tesco strives to support local communities and environmental initiatives, such as trialling zero emission home delivery vans, using bagless dotcom deliveries, and raising £53 million for Cancer Research UK through Race for Life in 2006.

For graduates this means being part of a corporately and socially responsible organisation. It also means the potential for rapid progress and early responsibility across the Tesco business – including office, stores and distribution programmes.

Graduates get involved in everything from sourcing and tasting prospective products, to negotiating prices with suppliers. From predicting sales forecasts for acquiring land, to developing board presentations. Within three to five years, graduates could even be running a depot, or managing a large store.

The graduate programmes offer structured development with regular reviews and annual career planning. The training involves hands-on experience, and technical and behavioural development, supported by a mentor. Graduates are supported every step of the way, but it's up to them to maximise these opportunities and drive their own progression.

Tesco is interested in graduates from every discipline, who combine people management and analytical skills with the character to succeed in a constantly changing business. Full of fresh ideas, they need to demonstrate leadership to become a senior manager and show energy, enthusiasm and passion for the Tesco business.

Bright ideas.

Our graduates come up with lots of them.

You'll get plenty of responsibility.

Hands-on commercial experience.

And the chance to make important decisions.

So, wherever you join our business.

In head office, stores or distribution.

We'll make sure you're always, well... switched on.

To find out more go to **www.tesco-graduates.com**

Buying, Corporate & Legal Affairs, Corporate Purchasing,
Distribution Management, Finance, Food & Product Technology,
Human Resources, IT, Marketing (including Customer Research
& Analysis), Pharmacy Pre-registration, Property & Engineering,
Research & Analysis, Supply Chain, Store Management,
Support Office and Tesco.com

Transport for London

www.tfl.gov.uk/graduates

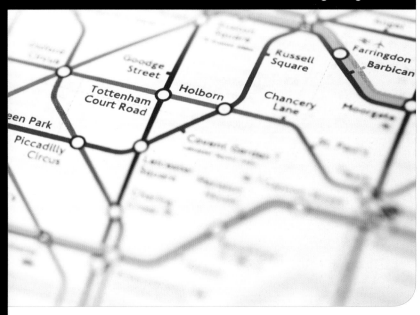

Vacancies for around 130 graduates in 2008

- Accountancy
- Engineering
- Finance
- General Management
- Human Resources
- IT
- Logistics
- Purchasing
- Research & Development

Starting salary for 2007
£23,000

Universities that Transport for London plans to visit in 2007-8

Bath, Bristol, Cambridge, Cardiff, City, Durham, Edinburgh, Hull, Leeds, Leicester, Liverpool, London, Loughborough, Newcastle, Oxford, Reading, Sheffield, Southampton, Warwick
Please check with your university careers service for details of events.

Application deadline
See website for full details.

Contact Details
✉ tfl.graduates@reed.co.uk
☎ 0845 241 4928

Turn to page 224 now to request more information about Transport for London.

Transport for London manages, develops and integrates the capital's transport network. That's everything from buses, roads and the Tube to taxis, trains, cycle paths and the river. They are a unique organisation.

Few other UK bodies have the responsibilities they have. Few other businesses have such a visible and far-reaching affect on the quality of life in London. Transport for London touches the lives of everyone who lives in, works in, or visits the capital.

And this is a particularly exciting time to join the organisation. Record levels of investment are fuelling the transformation of large parts of the network. London Underground is undergoing one the most exciting periods of renewal in its history. The demands of planning for a city that is predicted to keep on growing require foresight, innovation and imagination. And the 2012 Olympics will be a showcase not just for the best athletes in the world, but the best urban transport system too.

The graduate disciplines Transport for London recruit in range from technical to managerial to strategic to corporate. They take in the whole transport network, from underground to overground via the Tube, buses, streets and rail. All kinds of people work there. Engineers and information management teams. Business analysts and transport planners. HR teams and project managers.

So whatever the graduate scheme, successful applicants will be contributing to Transport for London's vision of a twenty-first century, state of the art transport network. A network that Londoners can be proud of and everyone who visits impressed by. A network that will set the standards others follow.

Imagine developing a transport system for millions of people.

Imagine keeping it safe, fast and reliable.

Imagine a graduate scheme that lets you.

Now stop imagining.

Graduate Opportunities within Transport for London

We have opportunities to suit graduates from a wide range of backgrounds across our organisation. So join us on the journey. Full details of all the schemes and how to apply are at **tfl.gov.uk/graduates**

We want to be as diverse as the city we represent and welcome applications from everyone, regardless of age, gender, ethnicity, sexual orientation, faith or disability.

MAYOR OF LONDON

Transport for London

**Vacancies for around
250 graduates in 2008**

- Finance
- Human Resources
- Investment Banking
- IT
- Logistics
- Research & Development
- Sales

Vacancies also available in Europe,
the USA and Asia.

Starting salary for 2008
£Competitive

**Universities that UBS
plans to visit in 2007-8**
Please check with your university
careers service for details of events.

Application deadline
4th November 2007

Contact Details
✉ sh-ubs-campusrecruiting@
ubs.com

Turn to page 224 now to request
more information about UBS.

UBS is one of the world's leading financial firms, serving a discerning international client base. Its business, global in scale, is focused on growth. As an integrated firm, UBS creates added value for clients by drawing on the combined resources and expertise of all its businesses.

UBS is the leading global wealth manager, a top-tier investment banking and securities firm with a strong institutional and corporate client franchise, a key asset manager and the market leader in Swiss commercial and retail banking. UBS employs around 80,000 people. With headquarters in Zurich and Basel, UBS operates in over 50 countries and from all major international centers.

It's what the employees do that makes UBS a leading global financial services firm. A graduate's skills, ideas and ambition drive the achievement of outstanding results for UBS clients and businesses. A graduate's personality and intellect are more important than academic discipline. At every stage of a UBS career, top-quality education and development resources support graduates in achieving their goals. UBS's world-class training captures potential and helps graduates hit the ground running. Ambition and application determine the speed at which graduates progress.

UBS's global client relationships are built on intimate understanding, so views and opinions are important. As a graduate's insights advance UBS's capability as a world-class enterprise, they contribute toward the decisions that power UBS growth. Above all, UBS wants graduates to be successful. The alignment of career aspirations and business objectives promotes the creation of lasting value for both graduates and UBS.

With your potential, our future is in good hands. It starts with you.

Your ideas make a difference. At UBS, we believe in creating opportunities for every one of our employees to empower them to excel and realize their potential. We know that the best view could be through your eyes. That is why we value diversity and want to create an environment that encourages different perspectives. As a leading financial firm with offices in over 50 countries, UBS can offer the inspiration you need from all corners of the globe. After all, when you're inspired, we all succeed.

It starts with you: **www.ubs.com/graduates**

Wealth Management | Global Asset Management | Investment Bank

You & Us

UBS

Unilever

**Vacancies for around
50 graduates in 2008**

- Engineering
- Finance
- IT
- Marketing
- Research & Development
- Sales

We believe 'dirt is good.'
Not surprisingly we're looking
for people who aren't afraid
to get their hands dirty.

**Starting salary for 2008
£26,000**
Plus benefits.

**Universities that Unilever
plans to visit in 2007-8**
Aston, Bath, Birmingham,
Cambridge, Durham,
Edinburgh, Leeds, London,
Manchester, Nottingham,
Oxford, Sheffield,
Strathclyde, Warwick
Please check with your university
careers service for details of events.

**Application deadline
December 2007**
See website for full details.

Contact Details
enquiry@
unilevergraduates.com
☎ 0870 154 3550
Turn to page 224 now to request
more information about Unilever.

Unilever is a leading consumer goods company, making and
marketing products in the foods, home and personal care
sectors across the world.

In fact over half the families in the world use brands such as Dove, Magnum,
Knorr, Persil and Lynx every day. Unilever's mission is to add vitality to life
– by helping people feel good, look good and get more out of life. Behind
every successful brand lie a number of complex challenges, in all areas of
the business: these are what graduates at Unilever will tackle.

Unilever's Graduate Leadership Programme is designed to help graduates
reach senior management. Graduates join a specific function in Unilever,
where they have a real job with key deliverables and responsibilities from the
outset. Generally, the scheme includes four placements within two years
therefore mobility is essential to achieve the breadth of experience required.
There is excellent training covering leadership development, general business
and professional skills. Full support is offered to gain Chartered status or
relevant professional qualifications, such as CIMA, IMechE, IChemE and IEE.

Unilever wants people with the potential to lead its business. To do this,
graduates need to be passionate about business, inspired by profit,
competition and customer satisfaction, as well as have the ability to behave
with integrity showing both ambition and entrepreneurial spirit. Unilever's
high quality training programmes help graduates develop the expertise and
personal qualities they need in order to achieve their career goals. They offer
a vast range of opportunities that just have to be taken.

For more information, please visit www.unilever.co.uk/careers

Fancy a challenge?

Unilever Graduate Leadership Programme

At Unilever we're responsible for producing some of the world's most popular food, home and personal care brands. So if you've got a big appetite for success, you'll find our range of opportunities a truly mouth watering prospect.

Whether you join us in **Supply Chain, Marketing, Customer Development, Innovation & Technology Management, Financial Management** or **Information Technology** you'll benefit from world-class training; you'll gain a range of experience from up to four work placements; and you'll develop all the skills you need to become a future business leader.

So think: could you get stuck into the challenge of making well-loved brands like Lynx, Dove, Walls, Flora, Persil and Ben and Jerry's even more popular? Could you hold your own with some of the most talented, creative and inspirational people in the industry? If so, you could soon be looking forward to a exciting career. Hungry for more? Visit www.unilever.co.uk/careers

Could it be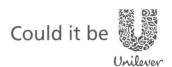

WPP

www.wpp.com

Vacancies for around 1-10 graduates in 2008

 Marketing
Media

Starting salary for 2008
£Competitive

Universities that WPP plans to visit in 2007-8
Bristol, Cambridge, Edinburgh, London, Nottingham, Oxford
Please check with your university careers service for details of events.

Application deadline
21st November 2007

Contact Details
✉ hmiller@wpp.com
☎ 020 7408 2204
Turn to page 224 now to request more information about WPP.

WPP is one of the world's leading communications services groups, made up of leading companies in advertising; media investment management; information, insight & consultancy; public relations & public affairs; branding & identity, healthcare communications, direct, digital, promotion and relationship marketing, and specialist communications.

WPP companies provide communications services to clients worldwide including more than 300 of the Fortune Global 500. Collectively, WPP employs 100,000 people in over 2,000 offices in 106 countries.

WPP Marketing Fellowships, which develop high-calibre management talent with experience across a range of marketing disciplines, will be awarded to applicants who are intellectually curious and motivated by the prospect of delivering high-quality communications services to their clients. All applicants should have completed an undergraduate (class 2:1 or above) or equivalent. Those selected will work in a number of WPP companies and across different marketing disciplines.

WPP is offering several three-year Fellowships – a unique multi-disciplinary experience, competitive remuneration and excellent long term career prospects within WPP. It wants people who are committed to marketing, who take a rigorous and creative approach to problem-solving, who are intellectually curious and will function well in a flexible, loosely structured work environment.

Each year of the Fellowship is spent working in a WPP sponsoring company and a personal mentor is assigned to provide overall career guidance. Each rotation is chosen on the basis of the individual's interests and the Group's needs.

WPP

Marketing Fellowships 2008

Ambidextrous brains required

WPP is one of the world's leading communications services groups. Major brands include JWT, Ogilvy & Mather Worldwide, Y&R, Grey Worldwide, The Voluntarily United Group of Creative Agencies, MindShare, Mediaedge:cia, MediaCom, Millward Brown, Research International, KMR Group, OgilvyOne Worldwide, Wunderman, 141 Worldwide, Hill & Knowlton, Ogilvy Public Relations Worldwide, Burson-Marsteller, Cohn & Wolfe, CommonHealth, Sudler & Hennessey, Ogilvy Healthworld, Grey Healthcare Group, Enterprise IG, Landor, Fitch and G2 among others.

Their specialist skills include Advertising; Media Investment Management; Information, Insight & Consultancy; Public Relations & Public Affairs; Branding & Identity; Healthcare Communications; Direct, Digital, Promotion & Relationship Marketing; and Specialist Communications. They are all in business to contribute to the success of their clients. And they do so through a demanding combination of flair and slog; intuition and logic; left brain and right brain.

We are looking for people who are intellectually curious and motivated by the prospect of delivering high-quality communications services to their clients. Those selected will work in a number of WPP companies and across different marketing disciplines. Excellent long-term career prospects within a WPP company.

Information leaflets are available from:
Harriet Miller at WPP, 27 Farm Street, London W1J 5RJ
T +44(0)20 7408 2204 F +44(0)20 7493 6819
E-mail: hmiller@wpp.com

Deadline for entry: 21 November 2007
visit our website and apply online at
www.wpp.com

Enter our prize draw to win £5,000 in cash or an iPod Nano (PRODUCT) RED!

Make use of our free information service to find out more about the employers featured within this edition of **The Times Top 100 Graduate Employers,** and you could be £5,000 richer when you start your first job!

All you need to do is complete the special Top 100 **Information Request** card that appears opposite and send it back before the final closing date, **31st March 2008**.

Or you can register your details online at **www.Top100GraduateEmployers.com**

Every completed request card or online registration will be entered into a special prize draw to win the £5,000 in cash.

There are also **50 (PRODUCT) RED iPod Nanos** from Apple to be won – one at each of the universities at which the Top 100 book is distributed, for those who reply by **30th November 2007**.

The information that you request will be despatched to you from the Top 100 employers directly. This service is entirely free to all UK students and recent graduates.

Fill in the card or go to www.Top100GraduateEmployers.com now!

THE ⚜ TIMES

TOP 100

GRADUATE EMPLOYERS

INFORMATION REQUEST 2007/2008

To request further information about any of the employers featured in The Times Top 100 Graduate Employers and enter our free prize draw to win £5,000, just complete your details and return this postcard.

Your information will be despatched to you directly from the employers, either by email, post or text message.

NAME _____

UNIVERSITY _____

COURSE_____

TERMTIME ADDRESS

_____

_____

_____

_____

EMAIL_____

MOBILE TEL. NO. _____

❑ PRE-FINAL YEAR   ❑ FINAL YEAR   ❑ I'VE ALREADY GRADUATED

The closing date to request information from these employers and be included in the prize draw to win £5,000 is **Monday 31st March 2008.** If you do **not** wish to be included on our general mailing list and receive information from other relevant graduate employers, please tick here ❑

Please tick the sectors that you would most like to work in:

ACCOUNTANCY.............. ❑
CONSULTING............... ❑
ENGINEERING.............. ❑
FINANCE.................. ❑
GENERAL MANAGEMENT .... ❑
HUMAN RESOURCES........ ❑
INVESTMENT BANKING ...... ❑
IT....................... ❑
LAW..................... ❑
LOGISTICS................ ❑
MANUFACTURING.......... ❑
MARKETING............... ❑
MEDIA................... ❑
PURCHASING.............. ❑
RESEARCH & DEVELOPMENT ❑
RETAILING................ ❑
SALES................... ❑

Please tick the organisations you would like information from:

ABN AMRO................. ❑
ACCENTURE................ ❑
ADDLESHAW GODDARD...... ❑
ALDI..................... ❑
ALLEN & OVERY............ ❑
ARCADIA.................. ❑
ARMY.................... ❑
ASDA.................... ❑
ASTRAZENECA............. ❑
ATKINS.................. ❑
BAE SYSTEMS............. ❑
BAKER & MCKENZIE......... ❑
BANK OF AMERICA......... ❑
BARCLAYS BANK.......... ❑
BARCLAYS CAPITAL....... ❑
BDO STOY HAYWARD....... ❑
BLOOMBERG.............. ❑
BP...................... ❑
BT...................... ❑
CADBURY SCHWEPPES...... ❑
CANCER RESEARCH UK...... ❑
CAPGEMINI............... ❑
CITI.................... ❑
CIVIL SERVICE FAST STREAM.. ❑
CLIFFORD CHANCE......... ❑
CO-OPERATIVE GROUP...... ❑
CORUS.................. ❑
CREDIT SUISSE............ ❑
DELOITTE................ ❑
DEUTSCHE BANK........... ❑
DLA PIPER............... ❑
ERNST & YOUNG........... ❑
EVERSHEDS.............. ❑
EXXONMOBIL............. ❑
FABER MAUNSELL.......... ❑
FINANCIAL SERVICES AUTHORITY . ❑
FRESHFIELDS BRUCKHAUS
DERINGER................ ❑
FUJITSU................. ❑
GCHQ................... ❑
GE..................... ❑
GLAXOSMITHKLINE......... ❑

GOLDMAN SACHS........... ❑
GOOGLE................. ❑
HBOS HALIFAX BANK OF SCOTLAND . ❑
HSBC................... ❑
IBM.................... ❑
JOHN LEWIS.............. ❑
JPMORGAN............... ❑
KPMG.................. ❑
L'ORÉAL................. ❑
LINKLATERS.............. ❑
LLOYDS TSB.............. ❑
LOVELLS................ ❑
MAERSK................ ❑
MARKS & SPENCER......... ❑
MARS.................. ❑
McDONALD'S RESTAURANTS.. ❑
McKINSEY & COMPANY....... ❑
MERCER................ ❑
MERRILL LYNCH.......... ❑
METROPOLITAN POLICE...... ❑
MI5 – THE SECURITY SERVICE . ❑
MICROSOFT.............. ❑
MORGAN STANLEY.......... ❑
NGDP FOR LOCAL GOVERNMENT . ❑
NHS.................... ❑
NPOWER................ ❑
OXFAM................. ❑
PENGUIN............... ❑
POLICE HPDS............ ❑
PRICEWATERHOUSECOOPERS . ❑
PROCTER & GAMBLE........ ❑
REUTERS............... ❑
ROLLS-ROYCE............ ❑
ROYAL BANK OF SCOTLAND GP . ❑
SAINSBURY'S............. ❑
SHELL.................. ❑
SLAUGHTER AND MAY........ ❑
TEACH FIRST............. ❑
TESCO................. ❑
TRANSPORT FOR LONDON.... ❑
UBS................... ❑
UNILEVER.............. ❑
WPP.................. ❑

THE INSTITUTE OF CHARTERED ACCOUNTANTS IN ENGLAND & WALES ❑